Disrupting **HR**

An Introduction to a New HR Doctrine

by David L. Garza

ISBN: 1481175718
ISBN 13: 9781481175715
Library of Congress Control Number: 2012923151
CreateSpace Independant Publishing Platform
North Charleston, South Carolina

Foreword

If you are in a position to influence the structure, design, and approach to the human resources department and function within an organization, this book will be of interest to you. Many successful companies are already seeing huge improvements after making changes to how they practice human resources; this book and the easy-to-implement strategies it contains will assist you in stimulating healthy growth in your own company. Following the establishment of the personnel department and its evolution into the human resources department in the past century, we are at the precipice of the next evolutionary step in the HR field's development in these opening decades of the new century.

As an HR executive, too often I have found that most of my personal time and effort, as well as my department's resources and capabilities, were absorbed by the administrative and transactional minutiae of day-to-day HR operations. You may smirk and say, "Well, of course!" As an HR executive, it is your primary responsibility to oversee HR and its administrative dealings to serve the organization. And, when I say transactional, it entails all of HR's functions, from benefits planning to compliance administration to compensation planning to employee relations' investigations to staffing requirements and so on. But in a day and age when so much administrative work can be automated or outsourced, why do organizations continue to employ the conventional HR model with a suspect cost-benefit ratio? To exacerbate the frustration further, it is also nearly impossible to evaluate the competitive advantage HR yields to an organization in business terms.

I am not stating that these traditional HR functions, services, and offerings are not needed. On the contrary, they are ever more important to an organization's existence, particularly in a marketplace where competitiveness has been accelerated through technological advancements and new economic conditions. However, I am challenging the context within which these services and offerings are deployed. That is, I have witnessed HR departments become omnipotent in how they serve their organizations to the point that they perceive their existence as essential and above the needs of the business. I have seen HR become regarded as an adversary, rather than a contributing, strategic arm of a business's strategy and goals. In worse cases, HR is viewed as just an administrative necessity where no competitive or strategic value of thought or action can be derived. So what's wrong with HR?

This book entertains a unique repositioning of HR as a much more participative function and contributor to the organization's ability to be competitive in its marketplace. It describes a reshuffling of the resources at hand with a renewed focus on people and how to engage the organization and the stakeholders it supports. Notwithstanding, it requires an open mind to what the future may hold for HR. The calamity of the Great Recession has changed the workplace. Wistful agnostics refusing to accept new realities still wait for a return to normalcy in the economy, but much like with every other significant historical event, life has been transformed. As the causes of the events that transpired were generated from decisions within executive boardrooms, there is an opportunity to correct our course. However, the days of free-flowing credit, wanton spending, and lack of accountability that sparked the Great Recession and drove organizational success has ended, and businesses must find a path to adapt and survive. Doing more with fewer resources to generate a profit is the short-term strategy. HR must find a way to contribute. It is my intent to present a view from the trenches with innovative ideas to help move HR to contribute to the effort while leveraging an organization's most important resource—its people.

- David L. Garza
Frisco, Texas

Contents

Preface

In 2008, I was fortunate to have been asked by a visionary CEO to join in his effort to change his organization's culture. His company was in the consumer goods industry with a recognizable brand identity. Even though the CEO explained that the HR department was in need of leadership, I hoped that I would finally be leading an HR function that was contributing to the organization's success much more than the previous HR departments I had assumed responsibility for in my past. Given the size and scope of the organization, I thought the HR department had to be well organized with a solid purpose. Despite the personal satisfaction gained from transforming an HR department, I was eager to find a department that was doing it "right." Despite warnings from the executive recruiter that the culture was very challenging, I believed that I could make an impact and that I would finally be working in a progressive HR organization.

Unfortunately, my hope dwindled shortly after my arrival when I realized that I was inheriting an HR function much like my prior leadership roles. The HR function was heavily vested in the administrative and transactional aspects of the field. When soliciting my executive peers for feedback about HR's interaction with their departments, the feedback was not much different from what I had heard in the past. The accounting department thought HR was nonresponsive, the operations department thought HR was adversarial and at times an obstacle, the finance department thought HR was incompetent, and so on. Despite my initial frustration, my duty was to bring HR into the organizational fold by transforming it into a department that could bring greater value to the organization and its people.

After more than two years of progress, the CEO left the organization, leading to my premature departure some two weeks later with unfinished work left in the transformation. I found myself looking for my next opportunity while thrust into the middle of a slow economic recovery. In those first few weeks of transition, I spoke with some of my HR peers and found that their experiences were very similar to mine in that they themselves were frustrated with HR's perception and an overemphasis on administrative and transactional duties and expectations. It was then that I realized that the utopian HR organization I sought was possibly a phantasm. As I researched HR in addressing this reality, I found only pockets of information about the problem and the opportunity. So, I felt compelled to address this persistent HR dilemma. That led to the writing of this book.

Twenty-five years of leadership experience and more than fifteen years of specific HR leadership experience, including front-line to executive roles, has shown me how effective and ineffective HR can be. Armed with the perspective gained through my work experience and an education that includes a BS in engineering with a focus of study in organizational behavior and leadership from West Point and an MBA from the McCombs School of Business at the University of Texas at Austin, I believed that I could do more good by sounding the alarm about HR's limitations and its potential than by sulking about its current state.

In the context of this book, I outline what I believe is undermining HR from a layman's perspective and what HR must do to become more engaged with the organizations it supports. I do this through the introduction of a new HR doctrine. As this is a doctrine, its purpose is to provide a guide for those who seek a new path. Many others have differing opinions and ideas about HR's past, present, and future, and I do not assume to be a voice for all HR professionals as many HR organizations are performing well and in alignment with what their organization demands. But, through my unique experience, I consistently observed under-potentialized HR departments, without a long-term outlook and possessing a negligible understanding about its potential to create success. This book presents an opportunity to unlock HR's potential.

- David L. Garza
Frisco, Texas

Acknowledgments

This book could not have been written without the help of so many. Foremost, I must acknowledge and thank my wife, Ellen, and my sons, Michael and John, for their patience as I worked through this writing project while exploring my career options.

Second, I must also extend my appreciation to Juan Fernando Roche, Sandra Stevens, and Nancy Loewe for their candor in providing me both input along the way and feedback as first readers of my manuscript. I must also thank Michael Blatz and Jasmin Brand for their contribution in helping me with their ideas and opinions.

I must give special thanks to Todd Hickerson, a great friend, a rival Annapolis graduate, and the architect of the human sustainability concept, for his detailed editing and for his contributions of ideas and suggestions that finally made this book complete. His wisdom and clarity were much needed.

Finally, my heartfelt thanks to the many HR professionals that I worked with along the way who endured my direction and approach that seemed to go against the grain, for through this experience I gained invaluable wisdom and perspective.

Part I:
The New Economy and the HR Gap

Chapter 1

The Great Recession:
Impact and Opportunity

Patrick, a vice president of human resources (VPHR) at ABC Company, had lunch with Clara, a well-networked outsourcing consultant. Clara mentioned that she had recently met with Carolyn, a highly placed executive with XYZ Company, a competitor of ABC Company. When Clara had mentioned ABC Company to Carolyn, her immediate response had been, "They are eating our lunch!" Carolyn shared that her company was consistently losing market share to ABC Company, except in smaller markets.

In the same week, Patrick met with a friend who talked about how his company had leveraged a major overnight express company to introduce his product into smaller markets that were off the beaten path and cost-prohibitive to support in-house. He said that his company was able to open a new revenue source at a low cost with the concept. As Patrick remembered that XYZ Company was succeeding in smaller markets, he realized an opportunity existed for his company to open a new revenue stream by using a third-party logistics (TPL) firm to expand the company's competitive product placement.

The next week, Patrick attended his company's weekly executive meeting as a fairly new member, having only a few months under his belt. When it was his turn to update the group on HR, he followed up his report by mentioning his conversation about the competitor's frustration and the idea to leverage the company's momentum using low-cost TPLs. The reaction was disappointing. The CFO snickered and mumbled under his breath to the head of innovation sitting next to him who then lashed out, "Since when is HR the source of business ideas in this company!" And with that, the idea was dismissed and the discussion moved on.

During the collapse of the world's financial markets in the early twenty-first century, few paused to ask where the human resources (HR) leader was in the midst of the regretful decisions and events leading up to the catastrophe. Granted, many of the decisions were made from behind closed doors by operational leaders and financial professionals and not likely by HR leaders. Hindsight is twenty-twenty, and these decision makers were not overly concerned with the potential fallout of their decisions on their organization's long-term existence. Rather, they were primarily concerned with growing the business's revenues for the present well within the scope of their responsibilities and interests. However, within the financial industry, particularly in the mortgage sector, professionals were later found to have entered into the sub-prime mortgage morass not through careful analysis and decision making but because everyone else was doing it and profiting.[1]

Once an organization's leaders decide to follow an unscrupulous path, if the HR leader challenges the direction it could have harrowing consequences to his or her career. Nonetheless, within the executive boardrooms of the companies that led the American economy into an unprecedented economic stall, HR professionals should wonder if the HR leader was in a position to influence and prevent the fateful decisions within these organizations from the onset.

As the question may never be formally investigated and less likely answered, in an attempt to explain HR's apparent absence from influencing the business events that led up to the Great Recession, three theories are offered. First, HR did not exist as a formal role to influence the decisions. Second, HR had the business knowledge, understood the consequences, and was complicit with the strategy and direction taken that contributed to the unfortunate global recession. Or, third, HR was not involved in the strategy because of being relegated or self-deposed to an uninvolved support or peripheral role.

As companies both small and large participated in the sequence of events that led up to the collapse of the markets, it is reasonable to think that HR may not have existed as a formal role in many of them. It may be even less plausible that HR was complicit in creating the complex investment arrangements that doled out financial risk to unsuspecting investors around the globe. For the purposes of this book, it is the third assumption that is the basis for considering a different approach to HR's role and purpose in the post–Great Recession economy. HR may have attained a seat at the table, but how will business and emerging HR leaders optimize it in the new century's economy?

As in the vignette that opened this chapter, challenging the status quo and ensuring HR is heard can be difficult. Some executives view HR's seat at the table in a very limited perspective. This may be due in part to expectations formed by previous experiences, events, or outcomes that establish HR in an uninvolved or peripheral role or status. Some HR leaders have overcome this bias and have gained the respect and acceptance of their executive peers so that they are influential in the business discussion, but this exists in only a few organizations.

One very reasonable explanation for this limited perspective and expectation may be found in how HR is conceived and sustained. The function of HR consists of a wide range of specialties that can be daunting and complex to master. Synchronizing these various specialties within HR to create value for the business, not to mention coordinating efforts within the department, is a formidable challenge. The functions of an HR professional range in nature from administrative to transactional to relational to transformational. Most HR professionals begin their careers within a specialty area or in an administrative role. Throughout a career, the typical HR professional is able to develop within an HR specialty area, or across different HR specialties, to become an HR generalist—a jack of all trades, master of none.

The function is so broad and diverse that even the most senior HR leaders typically maintain specific strength areas while other areas are not as developed within their repertoire. Despite this apparent shortcoming, the most senior HR leaders ordinarily possess a strong leadership capability that enables them to compensate for these less-developed areas by properly identifying, staffing, and supervising specialized HR professionals in these functional areas.

As it typically occurs, the line that divides an HR professional's specialty strength is most often delineated between the inward- and outward-facing HR functions. That is, some HR professionals are drawn to the back-office administrative and transactional areas such as record-keeping, payroll, benefits, compensation, and compliance. Others are drawn to the more interactive relational and transformational functional areas such as employee relations, labor relations, organizational development, and staffing. Regardless of interest, the HR field provides both specialists and generalists an opportunity for professional certification by demonstrating a mastery of HR's body of knowledge. This further legitimizes the specialty and broader functional expertise. However, the HR professionals in each specialty area remain distinct and separate in executing their functions in the normal course of operations, interacting with other areas only in response to an unusual situation or event. As is common to other fields, the modus operandi is reactionary.

It is still important to evolve HR's seat at the table and rethink how HR integrates with business because the post–Great Recession economy will demand a more proactive and participative HR function.

Furthermore, HR professionals alongside academics work diligently to grow and develop expertise within the field and its specialty areas. This is invaluable to the evolution of the field. The establishment of a graduate degree in HR in the past few years has garnered the recognition of HR as a formal academic discipline beyond the standard HR course offered in business schools in the past. But even this momentum in advancing HR can create blind spots that may inhibit HR from influencing the business debate beyond the typical dialogue. That is to say that if HR professionals dedicate their efforts to the growth and sustainment of the HR field insularly, there is a likelihood of missing the forest for the trees. The conventional HR approach that has developed over

7

time, in how the function has been organized, how its talent has been developed, and how the field has been advanced, can create limitations in growing HR's influence at the executive table.

But why is it important for HR to grow its influence or its role at the table? Looking back, the likelihood of HR being able to disrupt the juggernaut of poorly conceived investment arrangements, over-zealous consumers, and inadequate regulatory oversight that contributed to the Great Recession is not a reasonable reality should a similar sequence of events transpire in the future. This is quite acceptable to assume. However, it is still important to evolve HR's seat at the table and rethink how HR integrates with business because the post–Great Recession economy will demand a more proactive and participative HR function.

The global economy landscape is quickly shifting. China has risen as a global economic power but also faces the inherent risks associated with a burgeoning economy. Europe is wrestling with its own survival as it collectively attempts to stave off financial collapse of the European Union by dealing with its less dutiful members. Japan is still enveloped in a long recovery from its own financial woes while also overwhelmed with the recovery from a significant natural disaster. All these events have significant implications to the American economy as low wages abroad make off-shore labor an enticing resource, Europe's financial entanglement can impact Wall Street fortunes, and American industrial supply chains intertwine globally. Closer to home, the Great Recession and its fallout is rewriting how the American workplace, or more specifically, how a company and its employees, will interact in the future.

All this has implications for HR's role in the new economy. But, before considering an alternative way of thinking about HR's role and function, it is necessary to remember how the American workplace has transformed over the years. This provides an appropriate context to explore the possibilities emerging from this cataclysmic economic event. The dynamic relationship between business and its employees has been significantly altered and it has tremendous business implications beyond HR.

Beyond the obvious impact of mass layoffs and high unemployment, the Great Recession has magnified and cemented four realities derived from two significant trends borne out of years of change. This will further complicate the landscape for both HR and business leaders as these realities will be challenging but also create opportunities to grow HR's influence in the business strategy.

To understand the first significant trend impacting the workforce dynamic, it is necessary to reflect on the American economy in the late twentieth century. The standard covenant between an employer and employee, which first took root during the Industrial Revolution, was the expectation of lifetime employment and full pensions. This began to wane in the 1980s. Due to economic conditions that included fallout from the 1970s inflationary pressure, growing trade deficits, and over-evaluations in the market that culminated in the infamous Black Monday of 1987[2], companies were forced to reflect on their business model to determine where opportunities existed to drive out cost and increase profitability. More noticeably from that point in time, Wall Street's influence within the boardroom was firmly established in a much more public light. As the growth of mutual funds and 401(k) plans solidified Main Street's link with Wall Street, investor demands for greater market value through higher profitability with an emphasis on cost cutting became more commonplace with boards of directors facing greater scrutiny. The immediate strategy of cost cutting translated into, in the opinion of some, the shortsighted strategy of identifying and reducing labor costs or effectively eliminating headcount.

The terms *downsizing, rightsizing,* and *RIFs* (reduction in force) entered our workplace lexicon as layoffs became widespread and, as could be expected, unwelcome by employees who were eventually displaced. Despite the understandable disappointment of employees, a broad cleanup of corporate headcount rolls was needed. Some companies, by tradition, carried large workforce populations but either no longer had a competitive business model that required it, had experienced excessive headcount growth that was not aligned with organizational needs, or had been straddled with ruinous labor union agreements that caused them to retain underperforming employees. Nonetheless, there was a drive to become more profitable and increase market value by containing costs and, largely, the cost-cutting strategy worked. At least it worked in the short term to satisfy investor demands.

Workforce reductions soon became a common fallback strategy for new CEOs and boards through the 1990s in order to enhance a company's market value to satisfy Wall Street analysts and investor pressure. As CEOs and boards became even more responsive to Wall Street analysts and shareholders' expectations, employee engagement eroded through the beginning of the twenty-first century as layoffs often caught employees off-guard. As senior executives administered the workforce as an accounting line on the general ledger that could be managed as an expense, employees subsequently lost faith and trust in their employers and began to perceive management as callous with a disregard for their organizational value. Late twentieth-century technological advancements created unprecedented efficiencies and increased productivity levels to the point that fewer employees were required. Consequent layoffs contributed to the strained relationship between management and workforce.

This relationship shift amplified two realities that are being entrenched by the Great Recession. As previously mentioned, the workplace transformation altered employees' level of commitment and loyalty, or engagement, with their employers. Where it does exist, a modest percentage of organizations have an engaged workforce. In contrast to the short-term financial advantages of headcount reductions resulting in a smaller workforce, a highly engaged workforce has a greater potential to generate long-term sustainable value in productivity, quality, and cost containment through its inclination to be efficient, effective, and creative.

Gallup Consulting cited in its work on customer engagement that companies that highly engage both their customers and employees realize a 240 percent boost to the bottom line and outperform their competitors by 26 percent on gross margin and 86 percent on sales growth.[3] A *BusinessWeek* article mentioned that Best Buy saw a $100,000 annual increase in sales for every 2 percent increase in employee engagement in one of its stores.[4] This value proposition has yet to be broadly realized as the tangible value of headcount reductions is easier to recognize on financial accounting statements than an engaged employee's output. Thus, larger established organizations have conservatively taken the reduction of cost to the bottom line in lieu of engaging and optimizing their workforce.

As many employers' headcount was reduced, so too was their capacity to innovate or improve their products, services, processes, or systems. There are notable exceptions to this line of thinking as some large and established companies continued to be innovative, such as Apple with its unique product lines and start-up companies that created innovative new niches like social media giants Facebook, Twitter, and LinkedIn that blossomed during the Great Recession. But for the most part, innovation outside the technological and the diminutive but recovering manufacturing sector in the United States is nearly nonexistent.

In a *Time* magazine article, it was cited in two reports from the Boston Consulting Group and the Information Technology and Innovation Foundation (ITIF) that the United States ranks number six and eight, respectively, in the world for spending on research, patents, and venture funding—a hard measure of innovation. ITIF further found that of the forty countries analyzed, the United States ranked last in innovation capacity from 1999 to 2009.[5] Thus, it can be assumed including headcount reductions as a financial strategy further undermines the employer–employee dynamic and stifles innovation. Employees in these circumstances are likely to be cynical and resentful of the organization and far less likely to offer ideas or suggestions. The long-term impact of labor cost containment practices may result in a perpetual decline for organizations that are unable to compete without new products and services or greater efficiencies. With the continued deterioration of the employer–employee dynamic, an organization's level of productivity, service, quality, cost containment, and innovation will be negatively impacted.

> ***Reality #1: Workforce reductions have created less-engaged workforces that diminish an organization's competitive advantages gained from its human capital, such as its intellectual, productive, and innovative capacities.***

The second reality is derived from history repeating itself as the Great Recession of the early twenty-first century is transforming the current generation just as the Great Depression of the twentieth century transformed an entire generation decades before. In the 1930s, survivors of the decade-long depression were more likely to save their income and spend frugally in anticipation of another great financial calamity during their lifetime. They were greatly loyal to their employers as their employment was not only a valued source of income, but also a source of their identity—their lifelong commitment. This was the employer–employee covenant of lifetime employment.

Similar to the 1930s workers, the post–Great Recession employees, as consumers, are paying down personal debt, reducing their spending, and some are saving more than ever before. However, the post–Great Recession employees, who amassed large amounts of material possessions in the years leading up to the financial collapse, are not viewing their employment relationship in the same manner as their predecessors. Rather, their employer–employee relationship is a means to an end. And that end, prior to the Great Recession, was a personal lifestyle that supported a desired identity.

The cynicism that was rampant after the RIFs of the previous three decades contributed to employees, primarily knowledge workers, shifting their commitment from their employer to their personal careers. The focus on personal careers coincided with a greater focus on personal lifestyle. The more ambitious, and usually the more talented employees, selectively chose and progressed through targeted companies to land jobs that served their best interests, attempting to time their job changes when they reached the highest possible job level with their current employer. It was common for talented employees to change jobs every two or three years and hold jobs with multiple companies over the course of a career, sometimes due in part to layoffs and in part to selective career moves. The revised covenant between employer and employee has resulted in a transient relationship of mutual convenience and benefit that will make hiring and retaining talent in the post–Great Recession economy more challenging.

But the greater effect of this transient employment relationship is the business disruption it causes, particularly in a time when every employee's output matters because of reduced headcounts. When an employee is lost to turnover, that individual often takes significant intellectual capacity with him or her as many organizations do not possess an effective method to gather an employee's knowledge or learned experiences. Even if training manuals exist, the nuances of processes, relationships, and systems learned by an employee has a value to enhance an organization's competitive advantage. As the competitive market evolves daily, an organization without a thorough and robust business recovery or succession plan for all critical positions finds itself at a disadvantage when market opportunities present themselves if its human capital is lost.

> ***Reality #2: In a reduced workforce scenario, the ongoing transient behavior of an organization's key talent will create business disruptions that will multiply the chances of delayed or missed opportunities in the competitive marketplace.***

A second significant trend that is being enflamed by the Great Recession is the front-line employee's perception that he or she is sacrificing more than management in the United States's recovery. As these employees view their value to the organization and compare their lot with the management professional, their perception may manifest into external threats to the organization.

Prior to the Great Recession, many organizations were finding creative ways to reduce their costs and increase their revenues and profits with fewer resources. Some companies sought new revenue streams from within existing client portfolios to leverage existing cost structures rather than increase spending in developing new products or clients. Organizations also relied on technology to develop less expensive methods to produce, market, and sell their products and services. This "more with less" operational shift in businesses enabled it to employ a smaller workforce.

Unfortunately, in conjunction with workforce reductions, the economic calamity of the Great Recession resulted in business leaders also shifting to survival mode. Freezing merit increases, eliminating bonus plans, compensating employees with lowered salaries and wages, providing fewer or no perquisites, and temporarily eliminating or permanently reducing 401(k) contributions became necessary actions for survival. These decisions to contain costs were vacantly accepted by most employees in the perceived exchange for secure employment amid the frenzy of mass layoffs that accompanied the recession. Furthermore, companies tasked employees to assume additional duties and responsibilities as well as work longer hours as a practical solution to offset the reduced headcount levels. The trend of higher employee expectations with lesser rewards by employers is sustainable for the short term, but prolonged use of this formula will drive two further unpleasant realities.

The third reality requires a brief overview of unions in the post–Great Recession economy. The Great Recession resulted in a backlash against unions, who had been suffering a significant decline since their heyday in the mid-twentieth century. Similar to the underlying causes of the Great Recession on the corporate side, excess and greed has been the catalyst for the union's downfall.

The labor pendulum has swung against unions in the midst of the economic conditions that were created during the Great Recession. However, lower wages, fewer merit increases, more work, and longer hours cause employees to perceive a widening gulf between the management class and the larger working classes. American politicians debate austerity measures of reducing deficit levels by cutting social programs. The political dysfunction in addressing this and other issues may continue to make affordable healthcare accessibility difficult for many workers, keep executive pay disparities unresolved, and unsettle the financial markets with regulatory uncertainty, an uncertainty that has led to some businesses' indecisiveness on how to proceed in the face of diminished economic activity. As many employees lost their retirement portfolio value along with their job security and their trust of Wall Street and corporate leadership, the employer–employee relationship is ripe for a negative backlash.

As has been seen with the unrest in the Occupy Wall Street movement across the world in 2011, front-line employees may perceive an injustice in their lot in life. These employees might be asking if their best interests were sacrificed to bankroll the recession recovery. Much less due to political party support or legislative empowerment, unions are positioned to receive a grassroots resurgence from frustrated workers. Workers who have tirelessly saved their earnings and worked harder and longer for less may feel that they are being exploited and that the management ranks have more access to wealth and healthcare in comparison to them and that unions are their answer. More sophisticated employee groups may find a renewed political voice through unions and revise the third-party representation model for decades to come.

As has been seen in the American auto industry, unions in their current form create a drag on an organization's competitive ability. But in a revised union model, rather than vying for better wages and benefits, union groups may take further steps to assume a greater ownership stake in companies. It can be expected that, should unions ultimately hold a majority ownership stake, they will take a greater active presence and influence in investor meetings and quite possibly in the managerial ranks and boardrooms. This has begun to transpire in the American auto industry with union workers now owning a share of their respective companies in addition to traditional collective bargaining agenda items. Time will tell if this yields better results than the old model.

Nonetheless, if a union majority–ownership model comes to fruition, the repercussions would be unprecedented. It is assumed that given the Great Recession's fallout, conservative union ownership would place employee job security as a priority over innovation and improvements. This low-risk approach could deteriorate a company's competitiveness over time and, eventually, undermine employee security. The end of American global economic dominance would be inevitable. This is an extreme view with broad assumptions about how events could transpire, but without management ensuring that its relationship with employees remains positive, any future is possible.

Reality #3: The sustainment of employee economic sacrifices made in the post–Great Recession leaves front-line employees exposed to resurgent union-organizing efforts.

Finally, in the period prior to and leading up to the Great Recession, employment litigation was trending higher. A 2009 Jury Verdict Research Report stated the most common cases were sex and race discrimination, but cases also included age and disability discrimination and wrongful terminations. In 2008 alone, the median award for all types of American employment-related claims rose 60 percent to $326,640 according to the report. The cost does not include litigation fees that can range from $200,000 and higher. Furthermore, employers lost 61 percent of discrimination cases, 67 percent of age discrimination cases, and 48 percent of disability discrimination cases.[6] In their drive to retain their job, lifestyle, and dignity, employees who believe they have been wronged are filing claims against employers when removed from employment. This is a further indication that employees are emotionally detached from the organizations that employ them and driven much more by self-interest. (Unfortunately, it was a similar self-interest of Wall Street's best and brightest who were entrusted to safeguard billions of dollars of investor assets that caused one of history's worst financial crashes in pursuit of personal gain.) Employers must grapple with the self-interest mood that pervades American culture as its every decision and action is under watchful scrutiny. This is further amplified given the revised work climate where employees see their employer as an adversary rather than an advocate.

> *Reality #4: Due to a growing resentment by employees of their employers as a result of perceived employee sacrifices and management's indifference, employment litigation will rise exponentially in the next decade.*

The realities presented are not new. However, the volume and impact of these issues have a strong potential to be amplified due to the Great Recession. This amplification means that the same conventional approach used by HR in stemming the impact of high turnover, labor dissension, and employee issues may not be enough. The Great Recession has transformed the workplace and the employer–employee covenant. HR has a seat at the table, but just being at the table is not adequate to the challenge at hand. The future of HR is at a crossroads and events will move the field in a different direction regardless of whether HR chooses to make a conscious effort to participate in that movement. These challenges generate the need for those in the HR field to consider a change in its conventional approach. That change is key to HR's influence expanding at the executive table for the ultimate survival of the organizations it supports.

Chapter Summary

The Great Recession has left its mark on business organizations and workforces. The employer–employee relationship had been redefined by previous financial maelstroms, but the recession is magnifying the rifts created. Specifically, mass layoffs to reduce headcount have left some employers with a loss of human capital and diminished employee loyalty. Also, employers are facing increasing risks from dissatisfied employees from third-party representation groups and employment litigation.

1. Did your organization lose any competitive advantage as a result of the Great Recession's impact on the workforce?
2. Is your organization facing employment-related risk more frequently or more consistently than before the recession?

Chapter 2

What's Wrong with HR?

An HR leader, Gary, had recently joined a consumer goods company. The company's largest department was its manufacturing operation, employing more than four thousand of the company's six thousand employees. Daniel, the operations leader, with seventeen years of tenure, led the department. While on-boarding, a senior HR director told Gary that Daniel was difficult to work with and held HR with little regard. Against her advice, Gary invited Daniel to visit two manufacturing plants with him.

In the first plant, Gary met the rather standoffish operations executive. They toured the plant that had been recently acquired and found it in a state of utter chaos and disrepair. Daniel frustratedly pointed out each item on the plant floor that did not meet his expectations. The tour concluded and they embarked on a lengthy drive to the next plant.

On the drive, Gary asked his operations peer many questions about his operation, department, people, and finally, about HR. As Daniel began to relax and trust Gary, he revealed that he had a poor relationship with HR. Each of his actions regarding employees were challenged and an impasse existed with his assigned HR director. He confided that HR's support was essential to executing and achieving his strategy and goals and the current situation prevented him from effectively accomplishing the mission.

Upon his return to the office, Gary asked his staff about HR's relationship with its internal clients, particularly operations. A plant HR manager revealed that due to a personal dispute a standing order existed from the previous VPHR to challenge and block all of operations' requests, decisions, or actions. Gary was also told that during his trip, the regional HR director assigned to the operations executive had told her HR team that the new VPHR was getting "too friendly" with operations, revealing himself as a "soft" HR leader who was going to be ineffective.

We must first examine the basis of the conventional approach to HR before we can look ahead at alternative approaches. HR's historical roots lay in the advancement of technology. The Industrial Revolution, based on technological advancements in production, began the shift from an agricultural-based economy to an industrial-based economy and the introduction of factory work. This translated into a multitude of jobs, as new industries needed large numbers of employees to operate the machinery and equipment of its companies. With this growth, a worker helped to administer the hiring and payment of a company's employees and thus the first HR job was created—most likely as an office or payroll clerk role. As businesses began to grow, the complexity of managing an organization's employees evolved as even more employees were added.

HR's first transformation, as it is defined in this book, occurred in the first half of the twentieth century when the greater volume of work and work-related issues that arose from employing a larger workforce outgrew the capability of a clerical role. For the growing organization, staffing requirements grew, record keeping became a necessity for financial accounting, and payroll administration became more complex with tax codes. The personnel department was created and laid the administrative and transactional foundation of the future HR department. Companies now had a committed department to administer the employment of people.

The second HR transformation occurred in the latter half of the twentieth century as developments in market competition, psychology, and law influenced change. Many of the United States's dominant industries' growth crested, and competition among companies within industries grew. The service industry began to grow as manufacturing ebbed. Employees were no longer an inexhaustible resource as they were at the beginning of the Industrial Revolution. Increased competitiveness warranted a more deliberate effort to attract, recruit, and hire people. Companies began offering benefits, such as health insurance, to differentiate themselves as employers of choice. Psychologists began to explore how humans worked and what motivated them to perform. Motivation theories surged, creating a wave of programs to recognize, reward, and engage people. Labor, employment, and civil rights laws required renewed hiring and employment practices. New laws required that employers protect and treat employees fairly and companies took an interest in preventing labor movements. Workforces became increasingly diverse as women surged into the workforce and minorities were given unprecedented access to greater opportunities. Personnel departments were reinvented into human resource departments and HR was recognized as a key contributor to a company's operation. HR professionals came together to establish professional associations whose efforts formalized HR as a credible field. As a result, HR began to form its strategy and structure based on its emerging functions. A typical HR organization became commonly structured around these basic HR functions or "centers of excellence" as shown in Figure 1.

To guide HR professionals in delivering value to the organization, HR and management consultant Dave Ulrich of the University of Michigan's Ross School of Business studied the field at length. Through his work, he codified HR's mission into four activities:

1) Align HR and business strategy
2) Re-engineer organization processes
3) Listen and respond to employees
4) Manage transformation and change[7]

HR reached a new pinnacle, and through its evolution, charted a trajectory that took it from back-office clerking to a seat at the executive table where it could provide substantial value to the organizations it supported.

As much as this narrative destined HR to a future of tremendous influence and contribution, HR's fulfillment of these noble expectations is questionable. In the view of some individuals, HR consistently has not delivered on its expectations across most industries in the US economy with some exceptions. *Forbes* magazine contributor Karl Moore wrote in a 2011 article that early in his career at IBM he "was taught that HR were people to be avoided, they generally got in the way and were

Figure 1. Core HR Functions

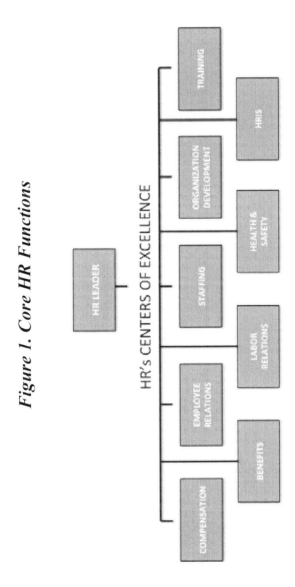

mainly paper pushers."[8] In 2005, *Fast Company*'s Keith Hammond wrote the article "Why We Hate HR" and argued, "HR is the corporate function with the greatest potential—the key driver, in theory, of business performance—and also the one that most consistently under-delivers."[9] Michael Blatz, former president of Lennox Corporation's Service Experts division, confided in an exchange about HR's strategic role that "many executive professionals are unclear on what they should be looking to their HR teams to provide and how to best use them."

With this level of discontent and uncertainty, there is something amiss between what HR has designed itself to provide and what it actually delivers. HR's success in getting a seat at the table has been a standing achievement lauded within the field as it represented a professional respect for the importance of human resources by other functional executives. It ushered forth the expectation that a firm's human resources department could be leveraged as a strategic differentiator. However, this achievement may be characterized as a "paper tiger" that was accomplished well before the end of the last century. As recently as the first decade of the new century, critics have voiced criticism about how the HR field at large has optimized this opportunity, as suggested by Moore and Hammond.

Some HR departments have undoubtedly earned these unappealing perceptions by design and by their own behaviors and actions. A myriad of laws, regulations, and program requirements demand attention, and at times, overwhelm HR departments with a slew of administrative work that consumes both time and resources. By virtue of this reality in some organizations, HR departments are perceived as nonpartisan and objective entities working in the periphery, rarely committing to positions or sides in business discourses; this projects an assumed neutrality. Some emerging HR leaders have inherited or developed this perceived neutral role effectively within an organization's leadership team. But others appear to use this as a convenience to refrain from participating in the firm's business strategy or from entering into discussions that have a significant impact to their organization. It may be because these topics lie outside their perceived scope of influence, control, or knowledge base. Ultimately, some in HR miss an opportunity to contribute meaningfully, as these leaders remain conservatively within their functional expertise and avoid venturing into broader business topics, resorting to employee advocacy or administrative compliance as HR's core purpose.

In a self-fulfilling prophetic sense, an organization's leadership group accepts the HR leaders' nonparticipant behavior and this further relegates these leaders to being noninfluential in the business dialogue and more consigned to administrative work. In these organizations, any later attempt by an HR leader to comment or participate in the business discussion is viewed as an inconsequential amusement as the HR role has already been cast. Thus, the perception of HR leaders as nonpartisan, objective, and administrative prevents them from ascending to a higher level of influence, contribution, and impact on an organization. Ironically, the most senior HR roles in some of the largest business organizations are being assigned to executives from other disciplines and functional units outside HR in part due to this lack of regard. This was witnessed at Yahoo Inc., where its newly assigned CEO, Marissa Mayer, selected veteran investment banker Jacqueline Reses, a proven leader who had never held an HR post previously, for the new position of EVP of people and development.[10]

However, even in organizations that select their HR leaders from the HR ranks, some of these leaders further add to a negative perception of HR. Sometimes HR leaders abandon any vestige of impartiality by aligning with or standing against a specific position or individual to promote a self-serving purpose. These HR leaders have an overzealous ambition and a highly political agenda often masked behind their well-spoken, well-pedigreed, and confident exterior. Despite their strong presence, they lack staying power due in part to a self-destructive arrogance, malevolence, and uncharitableness that undermines their effectiveness. Despite HR's perceived benevolent role, it is not immune from political individuals within its ranks. Where present, a politically motivated HR leader unfortunately adds to the negative perception that leaves many of HR's business peers wanting.

To widen the gap further between HR and the organization, some traditional HR professionals commonly form a function-centric viewpoint built around the previously mentioned core functions or centers of excellence. When overly developed, this viewpoint may at times form into an onerous, self-affirmation of HR's role within an organization's structure. It can often seem to individuals outside HR that from behind HR's castle wall and moat, HR professionals enforce their own set of edicts upon organizations using employee advocacy as a sword and compliance as a shield.

In its worst manifestation, this approach can paralyze the business as it did in the opening vignette of this chapter. In the story, the previous HR leaders had created a department that was an obstacle to the company through passive and active aggression, which disrupted the business flow. The department had become disconnected from the organization, adrift in fulfilling its own agenda. The new HR leader was perceived as a threat to the status quo and was being challenged from within the HR department's ranks to protect the existing state of affairs. This presents an extreme example of how HR can become detached from its mission, over-develop its role, and be of marginal value to an organization. Another example of this function-centrism is commonly witnessed by how HR emphasizes process as a priority over results. Most often seen in the staffing function, external recruiters and internal business leaders become critical of HR teams as their design and adherence to candidate selection processes extends longer than the candidate's "shelf life," overlooking the business need. As there are necessary steps to properly select a candidate, qualified candidates are lost to competitors at times because of an over-emphasis on process rather than a focus on fulfilling the business need.

This is not to say that the theory, laws, regulations, and advocacy that generate an HR-centric view should be sacrificed for the organization's interest, as a need does exist for a focus in these matters. But rather it is to say that the myopic, function-centric viewpoint limits the perspective taken by HR professionals and it can become a constraint in their ability to participate in the business discussion. Despite the constraint, there are positive yields from this function-centrism such as the centers of excellence that have honed the field's functional discipline. However, as HR delivers its services, advice, or consultation as requested or needed through these centers of excellence, these efforts may not be congruent with the organization's strategy despite the belief by HR leaders that they are aligned. This misalignment contributes to the frustration that business leaders hold against HR and prevents emerging HR leaders from ascending to a higher level of influence, contribution, and impact to the organization beyond HR. It serves to undermine the respect given to them by their functional peers and employees.

It's not just business leaders who perceive HR with a questionable view. Employees also struggle with their perception of HR by virtue of their relationship with the function. For employees, HR has two sides. One side is as an advocate in that HR assists employees with issues involving pay, benefits, or time off. On the other side, HR is sometimes seen as a bureaucratic adversary when enforcing company policies and delivering disciplinary actions to employees in a perceived disenfranchised manner. Employees may believe that they cannot exist without HR, but neither can they trust HR. Employees who are asked to come to the HR office at times conjure up a dead man walking idiom as such arranged interactions with HR are seen in a negative light. These perceptions have even transcended into our cultural narrative as HR has been portrayed in a less-than-positive light from comic book characters (Catbert in the *Dilbert* comics) to television portrayals (e.g., *The Drew Carey Show*).

Essentially, a sad irony is borne out in most HR-centric departments. Unfortunately, some HR professionals develop a cynicism about the employees they exist to support. That is, no employee can be trusted unequivocally to follow company expectations or to do the right thing for the company. This cynicism transpires over time as some HR professionals develop a belief that either employees are motivated by self-interests or simply do not care. This belief stems from a series of mostly negative interactions with troubled employees' issues or problems. Based on a human-motivation Theory-X belief that employees are not motivated to work, HR leaders and staff assume a company-protector and rules-enforcer role. Employees are viewed as the enemy as HR staff enact an unofficial but standing order to protect and enforce. Any errant behavior outside the box is viewed as a deviance from the norm regardless of intent, outcome, or impact. This is often demonstrated by how some organizations have developed a fervent disciplinary action process. This is often reinforced by employment law attorneys who advise with a guard against the various risks of employing people. However, there are overzealous lawyers who go beyond advising on risk and characterize employees in a less-than-favorable light that influence some HR professionals to form a strong negative view about the people in their charge.

In these punitive environments, discipline becomes the objective and administrative exactness is the preferred outcome to enhance the chances of opposing an employee claim filed against the employer. Despite the obvious benefit of containing risk and cost for an organization, this approach can at times stifle innovation and creativity as a police state can form that keeps all employees, and the rest of the organization, within the box. This enforcement culture at times contradicts the organization's best interests due to HR's misalignment.

HR promotes its existence from a self-validating drive that ultimately creates a peripheral distance between itself and the core business despite the appearance of being strategically aligned.

But why so much disdain for a department or function that has people as its core reason for being?

The answer to this question lies in the very foundation that HR has been built upon. Despite the tremendous efforts by HR professionals, consultants, professors, and associations to advance the field, HR has fallen victim to an incestuous approach. HR promotes its existence from a self-validating effort that ultimately creates a peripheral distance between itself and the core business despite the appearances of being strategically aligned. As a whole, the HR field generally continues to work within a context that neither expects nor demands its professionals to influence a different future for the HR field outside the accustomed HR realm. In attempts to find evidence of a new way of HR thinking, Internet searches for HR using terms such as "revolutionize," "innovative," or "progressive" yield consulting firm websites or articles about improving conventional HR products, services, competencies, and approaches or doing conventional HR better than the incumbent HR professionals. As it stands, innovating HR today is characterized by doing the same things as have been done in the past, only differently or better.

The HR field is at the precipice of its next evolutionary step, as the historical order of events will demand it. The HR field's conventional design, its intentions, its talent, and its leadership must change in that evolution to fulfill its potential in aiding organizations to succeed. Unfortunately, this viewpoint may be more commonly held outside HR and not readily recognized by those within HR. In its current state, many HR organizations operate with a conventional mindset that may fall short of the reality of the post–Great Recession's business environment and the revised employer–employee covenant. Given the complexity of managing a business to overcome the post–Great Recession challenges of low employee engagement, constrained innovation, increased litigation, rising union risks, and greater compliance, HR leaders must be prepared to step into the breach to assume a position that directly contributes to the recovery out of the Great Recession. Emerging and existing HR leaders must adapt to address these developing realities and transcend the limiting perspectives of the conventional HR approach. They must truly optimize their seat at the table by participating in, contributing to, and influencing the business discourse expected by business leaders.

To do so requires an analysis of potential underlying causes for HR's perceived nonparticipative behavior and function-centric myopia. HR's foundational core is derived from its expertise, leadership, advocacy, and motivation. Understanding the apparent causes within each area sets the platform for a new pattern of thinking.

Expertise

As previously alluded to, the HR field has been dutiful in developing its function. This development placed heavy emphasis on the functional and transactional aspects of the field. The attention and resources of HR professionals have been constantly focused inwardly on how to better function or transact to achieve more efficient or impactful results. Advances in systems, practices, and processes have created much-needed improvements. By developing the function, HR grew its capacity and contribution beyond its origins of clerical bookkeeping and payroll.

However, this development path has also created an inward mentality about the field's existence and purpose. Despite callings by HR theorists and consultants for HR leaders to become strategic thinkers or to be strategically aligned, many HR professionals primarily have done so within the context of their HR existence. If a strategic objective is to contain cost, some HR teams work to reduce cost within the function thereby rendering it strategically aligned of its own accord. Strategic thinking in HR has often been getting the most yield out of HR systems, coaching executives and managers on relationships, or managing vendor relationships to gain cost efficiencies. All this is good activity, but it still remains function-centric and limits HR's capacity to influence the business. This opinion should not be construed as an overall condemnation of these efforts, for without an element of centricity, HR could not have attained the heights that brought it to this point in its evolution. HR's centers of excellence and shared-services approach dominate the HR landscape and continue to be an important element in HR's future. Any evolutionary step forward requires a transactional excellence to serve as a foundation for a higher HR contribution level.

However, HR's progress to date cannot be the boundary that confines HR from reaching a future when it will enable organizations and their people to succeed rather than to just exist. HR professional expertise must expand beyond these self-made boundaries and empower the field to assume its new mission in the new economy.

30

Furthermore, and despite an initial exuberance, the establishment of graduate degrees in human resources represents an educational acknowledgement of the field's importance, yet these programs have the potential to further distance HR from the business dialogue. As mentioned, new HR professionals typically are assigned to an HR specialty area and eventually are presented the option to move into a generalist role or remain in their specialty area as they progress in their career. Regardless of path, HR professionals are immersed in HR's core tasks and duties daily. During this early career phase, HR professionals could take best advantage of a degree in a human resources–related field that provides broader academic context and foundational reference that supplements their day-to-day experiences. Gaining a professional HR certification early in their career also offers volumes of practical knowledge and insight into the HR field.

As HR professionals assume leadership roles at mid-career and beyond, their dealings expand outside HR. HR leaders begin interacting with functional business unit leaders with broader organizational issues in the balance. Knowing more about business and how it functions becomes essential to the HR leader's effectiveness. As some mid-career HR professionals decide to pursue an advanced degree to enhance their knowledge, a degree in a human resources–related field may not be what is most needed. Rather, a business-related degree is better suited to the developing HR professional's need for broader business understanding for impending HR leadership roles. That is not to say that advanced educational development in HR and its specialty functions is unneeded or unwelcomed, but it must be balanced in preparing HR leaders for a broader business role or it will hinder their contribution in the business operation.

Many HR professionals also need a comprehensive understanding of risk as it underscores the new economy's realities. Even though many HR professionals work closely with their legal counterparts to minimize or defend against legal claims filed against the organization (often in reaction to an event or situation through better investigation methods and documentation) or with safety professionals to prevent unsafe conditions, HR professionals sometimes underestimate the scope of risk that is associated with an organization's people. If overly managed, concerns over risk can harm or paralyze an organization with an overemphasis of conservative caution. If left unfettered, people risk can overwhelm an organization. People risks generally are derived through job-related activities:

- Human occupation: workplace injury, personal illness
- Human interaction: disengagement, workplace violence, third-party representation
- Human capital: loss of gained experience and knowledge
- Human capabilities: missing or inadequate skill and abilities for organizational evolution such as mergers and acquisitions in new industries or new technologies

Risk is a viable threat to an organization as it can negatively impact its financial and operational wellbeing if the above areas are not properly monitored or maintained. Failing to manage risk as a specialty function in and of itself leaves HR professionals exposed and negates their positive contributions to the organization.

An HR expertise with undeveloped business acumen and risk understanding undermines HR's effectiveness in engaging in the business dialogue. A function-centric expertise creates an artificial boundary that limits HR's influence and contribution and it must be addressed.

Advocacy

In many organizations, HR professionals are commonly designated as employee advocates through job descriptions, performance objectives, and professional discourse. And in those organizations with an enforcement culture, HR professionals are likely to advocate on behalf of the organization and for HR in upholding policies and rules.

The employee advocacy role that HR is tasked to fulfill misses its mark because of a misguided notion about advocacy. Being an employee advocate creates the expectation that HR must represent an employee's position in all matters. In an ideal state, all leaders should advocate on an employee's behalf in matters such as respect, health, and safety. But even in this broader advocate context, advocating for employees is only part of the equation.

Advocating for the company or an HR policy may in appearance seem to show a much more impactful application of advocacy. However, this approach confines an HR professional to defending a set of rules or guidelines that were borne from a need for control and not necessarily to augment an organizational purpose or strategy. Analogous to employee advocacy, all leaders should advocate a company's policies to promote desired values and behaviors. But this too is also only part of an equation of a broader advocacy role. In either role, many leaders and employees view HR as one-sided in their advocacy.

Furthermore, the outcome may not necessarily be in the best interest of the organization when measured by its contributive value to an organization's strategic and financial goals. Depending on the HR professional, many different paths can be taken to generate a resolution when issues arise between the organization and the employee. HR professionals generally will err on the side of the issue that most resonates with their disposition about their role and responsibilities, morals and ethics, and rules and guidelines. As most HR professionals place a reliance on their perception of HR's purpose, their experience, and their education to perform their normal duties, it is most likely their advocacy efforts will be limited to these influences as well.

Nonetheless, the advocacy role that HR assumes varies with the organization and its culture. For some HR professionals, it reinforces a perceptual distance between HR and its constituents.

Leadership

HR has to overcome leadership conventions that have developed over the course of time. In most organizations, HR's structure is hierarchal, similar to other business units. All primary HR specialty functions report directly to the HR leader. While this ensures a strong command

and control system so that the HR leader is fully aware of each specialty function's roles, responsibilities, activities, and outcomes, it also has the potential to promote a "silo" existence for the HR professionals within each specialty function. If a silo existence develops, next level HR leaders and professionals work autonomously, only communicating with other specialty function peers as necessary in department-wide meetings or collaborating in response to situations that arise. As senior HR leaders are consumed with day-to-day operations, it may be more an exception to find HR departments with cross-functional initiatives to develop their key HR talent. Circumstantially, the most opportunistic and most curious HR professionals learn about other HR specialty functions on their own.

The structure also reinforces a function-centric leadership style, somewhat necessary and common to all other departments. HR leaders commonly promote their department's interests as its top representative, competing with other departments for resources. By its very nature, a hierarchal structure emphasizes a focus on conducting internal operations. As with other support functions, HR provides its products and services primarily to internal organizational clients, and is structured for internal departmental effectiveness and efficiency to do so. The HR structure's emphasis on function influences HR to be internally focused on department demands and needs rather than externally on the business challenges being confronted by the organization in the new economy.

As suggested, HR's leadership approach and hierarchal structure points HR's leaders to serve HR's needs as they arise first and to keep the department's functions operating primarily apart from one another. Though HR is seen to be the department that serves the organization and its people, its leadership design suggests otherwise.

Motivation

Motive is defined as a reason for doing something and in this case a reason for engaging in one's occupation. It can never be said that HR is not motivated as a department. In fact, the number of HR tasks can be overwhelming and rarely is an HR professional at a loss for things to do as the anxiety of completing it all and doing it well is a motivating force. However, HR's motive as to why it performs its activity is open to debate.

Because of the centrist approach to developing the HR field, HR's motive lies between a validation of its own activity and an effort to support the needs of the organization. Some may argue that in essence all of HR's efforts and results support the organization, and to some extent this is accurate. However, it could easily be argued that HR's motivation may begin with the organization in mind but it ends with HR measuring its success against its own standard. As HR professionals develop HR's goals and objectives as a function, it can be considerably disassociated from the strategic business direction. Metrics such as time-to-fill rates, open enrollment completion rate, headcount full-time equivalent (FTE) to HR FTE, payroll error rates, and process adherence are reported by HR teams to the broader organization to substantiate HR's contribution and demonstrate a return on investment of the resources and effort expended. Yet, having the best possible score and ratings on these metrics may not coincide with the organization achieving its business strategy and financial objectives.

The completion of tasks and duties are essential to objective achievement. HR activity is not to be scorned as a waste of time, but it should also not be representative of progress against the business strategy and financial goals. Measuring HR activity is similar to monitoring professional baseball statistics. Regardless of a player's batting average, number of strikeouts by a pitcher, or runs scored in a game or in a season, it is the number of wins that the team can achieve that really matters in reaching the goal of winning championships. And, in the case of business, how much market share can be gained, revenue earned, cost contained, and profit made matters more than unaligned department metrics. This distinction is at times lost upon HR professionals that post activity levels as a measure of progress for the function. These efforts also further undermine HR in understanding its potential for a broader and more contributive role.

This issue is perhaps observed most in the HR specialty area with the greatest motive and opportunity to support the organization and its people in achieving success. It is also the functional area that is most often prevented from doing so by external forces as well as by its own accord. The organizational development (OD) function has a very appealing proposition to lead the effort for improving organizational performance as a change agent and organizational expert. However, OD practitioners often become mired in a fight for survival. This dilemma occurs in large part due to OD's need to validate their existence and value to the organization.

Because of perceptions about HR's overall functional value to the organization, OD programs and resources are often substantially impacted in cost-reduction exercises to streamline HR's budget. Typically, business leaders, and consequently HR leaders, do not regard OD as essential to sustaining business operations and will sacrifice it in favor of other HR functional areas, such as compensation, benefits, and payroll, in order to reduce cost or expenses.

These other transactional specialty areas are most often given priority not because of the strategic contribution they provide, but rather for their contribution in keeping the organization operating with minimal HR cost. In turn, many OD professionals are trapped into placing a heavy emphasis on the tools and measures of their work to validate their role. That is to say, for example, completing the employee engagement survey becomes the objective over the business improvement it has the potential to affect. This is not to say that all OD professionals initiate or complete programs on their own accord to justify their worth. Most often, business leaders request solutions for business problems relating to people from HR/OD first. But by demonstrating how successfully a program or tool has been implemented, OD is able to accomplish a measure of relevancy in order to protect its existence in the HR portfolio. This motivation to be relevant obscures many OD professionals' true aim with regard to their potential impact upon an organization.

Another problem facing HR/OD is that the tools and programs sometimes appear to other business unit leaders to have been designed with minimal business consideration. Despite being well meaning and scientifically well supported, psychological theory and business reality often become entangled in conflict between idealistic and practical divergences. Core OD programs, such as leadership development, employee engagement surveys, and performance management have become principal to HR/OD's effort but can also create distractions to organizational reality. Competing interests for resources—most especially time and money—at times makes OD's programs an inconvenient and inconsequential demand that raises the ire of business unit leaders. *Fast Company*'s comment by Keith Hammond about HR having the greatest potential in driving business performance yet under-delivering touches the nub of OD's quandary. The following examples demonstrate these relevant issues:

- Employee engagement surveys are designed to identify issues and concerns with employee groups that impact a workforce's engagement and are usually completed on an annual basis. It is supported by the theory that engagement directly affects performance. Surveys reveal topical areas in the organization with low engagement ratings. Typically, an organization attempts to address the issues by forming ad-hoc task forces to investigate, recommend, and implement solutions with the hope of improving the topical area that is to be measured again in the next survey. However, success is oftentimes measured by percent participation or by a rating improvement from rating period to the next rating period. Ad-hoc task forces become a chore for participants if unfocused rather than a resource for change for those involved. The problem is that organizations often fail to demonstrate the more important link between engagement and organizational and individual performance. Few OD professionals link engagement ratings to revenues, operating expenses, earnings, share value, risk, litigation, productivity, service levels, quality, and efficiency.
- An implied responsibility and duty of an effective leader is to develop next-level leaders. Succession management is the

program that is designed to assist leaders in this effort, but it can become an administrative OD exercise that many times does not fulfill its expectations. A succession management process can be an unavailing effort when it yields minimal impact to an organization's effectiveness, save for peace of mind and support for leadership development initiatives. Unfortunately, the process has the tendency to shift the focus from its intended purpose to its method. Ideally, an effective leader identifies and prepares future leaders by assigning roles and activities, clearing obstacles, and providing informal mentorship. More importantly for practical rather than developmental purposes, succession management is essential for continuity of operations in that the senior leader identifies his successor and those of his immediate staff for unplanned extended absences or departures. As organizations evolve and challenges arise, the relationships between a leader and his extended team can adequately address these challenges whereas a succession-planning grid, focused more often on individual development, misses the organization's immediate and short-term needs as a passive tool. Nonetheless, OD professionals dutifully take conscientious steps to evaluate and identify high-potential employees, guesstimate a readiness timeline for each individual, and recommend development opportunities that may or may not be realistic to the organization's competitive realities.

- Leadership development efforts range from off-the-shelf to customized programs that are generally designed with a mix of coaching, mentoring, business acumen, and soft skills training. Quite often, leadership development efforts focus on executives, senior, and middle management, and some efforts are in support of a succession management program. This conjures forth the idiom of closing the barn door after the horse has bolted or simply trying to take action when it is too late. Investing in leadership development for senior-level leaders who supposedly have been selected for their roles because of their demonstrated leadership qualities, assuming that the selection process employed was designed to do so, seems ineffectual. This opinion is underscored by a common reality that as leaders rise through the ranks, they come to recognize that the characteristics and qualities that they employed to advance in their career should also be applied in their next role. This makes it a challenge to develop leaders who, through their experience, have formed leadership beliefs and capabilities in which they are highly vested. Nonetheless, OD professionals are often tasked or choose to focus on senior leadership development, specifically when soft skills are absent. Oftentimes organizations maintain a senior leadership development program to demonstrate parity with other organizations that are highly regarded in the industry and to satisfy board expectations, yet its impact is difficult to measure. While the efforts are focused on senior and mid-level leaders, leadership development in the formative period of a developing career, most often at the level closest to the organization's customers or operations where it is most impactful, is often neglected or under-resourced.

- Broad criticism is being leveled upon performance reviews from both inside and outside of HR. The annual exercise seems to be minimally influential upon an individual's performance and is mostly valued for its use in compensation planning. Some organizations adopted the GE method and used performance management to drive out the bottom performers each year. Advancements in performance review tools have supposedly simplified the process but have nominally changed the fundamental design. Most annual reviews culminate on a specific date, typically at the end of the calendar year, and require a written analysis of the past year's performance, developmental opportunities, and a performance rating. This exercise is predominantly reserved for the managerial ranks, often ignored by the senior executive level, and rarely considered for the hourly workforce. As observed with the other previously mentioned OD programs, the performance review's impact on improving organizational and individual performance is rarely measured or validated. The review process suffers from inconsistency across the organization as some dutifully complete the process and others "pencil whip" the required forms. This makes compensation decision making challenging and performance improvement efforts inadequate. As a result, some organizations are abandoning annual performance reviews and experimenting with peer reviews or just forgoing it altogether.

Another contributing factor to OD's challenge is that OD professionals are immersed in the behavioral sciences in their academic endeavors. HR/OD leaders with an industrial-organizational (I-O) psychology degree have studied a robust curriculum that commonly includes courses on organizational change, development, assessment, learning, training, consultation, personality theory, communication, cultural dynamics, statistics, and research design. As this degree program is developed from a scientific perspective, a gap is formed between psychological theory and business reality.

As they assume their roles within organizations, many IO-educated OD professionals focus on applying learned behavioral and motivational theory and methods to influence individual behavior and performance. However, the science-to-business gap is exposed when some HR/OD professionals define their success in terms other than what is relevant to the business strategy or financial objectives. OD candidates' resumes oftentimes reflect a list of accomplishments based on the design and execution of OD programs without mention of its impact on the business results. For example, a search for a director of talent management revealed a candidate with a PhD in industrial/organizational psychology. The doctor cited as a significant accomplishment the percent increase of her company's year over year global management movement as a result of her redesign of the company's global succession management plan. Despite the increased movement, there was no mention of the program's impact upon the business that related to achieving a business or financial objective, improving customer satisfaction, or enhancing the firm's market or shareholder value. To the doctor's defense, her efforts may have impacted these areas but what was displayed as an accomplishment on her resume was a description of the program's activity—in essence, an activity performed and not a goal achieved. This is a unique example, but many OD professionals and organizations alike have come to practice OD in a manner that promotes the effort over the impact. This is further promoted from within some organizations and HR/OD departments as they post OD job openings with an education requirement of an I-O degree along with experience in designing and executing OD programs without a need to demonstrate business impact or results.

OD's motives are well intended in serving the organization, but factors shift the effort to validation or activity ahead of impact. This undermines the influence that HR and OD can have on the business organization, as these activities can be incongruous with the organization's broader needs.

Why should all of this matter? Because an ineffective HR function and people strategy creates an organizational dysfunction or friction. This friction has a cost and it can be substantial. Traditional methods have evaluated HR's impact to the organization by measuring turnover, employee engagement ratings, and workers' compensation costs. Realistically, HR has a greater impact to the bottom line in a much more direct manner:

- People inputs: skills, abilities, competencies
- People outcomes: productivity, quality, service, and efficiency
- People risks: lost human capital (by absence due to injury or illness or by turnover), litigation, third-party representation

If an ineffective HR function exists, then the potential exists for people to be hired with the "wrong" skills, abilities, and competencies. If this occurs, then individuals have the potential to create the "wrong" outcomes. An organization that fails to engage with its people also creates risk through low commitment and loyalty. This can impact the organization's market value by adding costs (inefficiencies or claim costs), reducing market share (poor product/service quality), and lowering profitability (lost revenue). If HR does not get the "right" people doing the "right things" in the "right" environment, it will negatively impact its organization in both seen and unseen costs. It is difficult to find research that links an HR function's effectiveness to the organization's profitability or market value. However, by observing Southwest Airlines, a company that built its business model by optimizing its people's talents, it is clear to see the potential that an effective HR approach and people strategy can have on an organization's business success. Finding a way to measure the financial impact of an effective people strategy through HR, all in the context of the organization's strategy, is HR's challenge in order to quantify its value and potential.

The HR profession must continue to maintain its transactional competence and objective stance, but it also must develop a greater strategic presence and alignment to help organizational leaders overcome the new challenges and realities to succeed. This greater presence and alignment is being defined within a new HR doctrine that disrupts conventional HR thinking. The doctrine does not fully replace the functional HR model, but rather leverages it. However, it requires an abandonment of the prevailing HR-centric perspective that permeates the profession.

To consider this new direction, today's HR leaders must volunteer to change their existing mindset about HR's role. They must consider the basic assumptions previously made about the limiting factors to HR that include both a function-centric and a nonpartisan approach to leading HR. Next, HR leaders must take an evolutionary step-by-step approach to establishing a new direction for the field. In the next section, a new direction is presented for transforming the HR function, beginning with a strategic outlook supported by principles necessary in enacting a new doctrine.

Chapter Summary

As a field, HR's self-perception differs from that of its business peers. HR may have reached a seat at the table, but some question if it is performing at its full potential. An HR function-centricity creates a myopia about its organizational role. As a result, HR is, at times, mis-aligned with the organization's direction. HR's expertise focus, advo-cacy beliefs, leadership structure, and motivation distractions contribute to this problem.

1. What is your organization's perception of your HR function?
2. What evidence can you find that your HR function is out of step with the rest of the organization?

Part II:
The New HR Doctrine

Chapter 3

Human Capital Optimization

A billion-dollar organization with five thousand employees had no formal talent acquisition function, process, or expertise at its corporate offices and had little oversight to the field's hiring efforts. Jeanne, a new HR leader, understood the importance of a talent acquisition program and the risk of not having a formal approach to hiring talent. To address the situation, she outlined a process and the needed tools to form the basis for a selection process that would require higher standards and a more stringent review of candidates. However, she still needed a manager to lead the effort. Unfortunately, no one in her immediate staff was qualified.

A few weeks prior, Jeanne had transferred Sabrina, an employee from another division, to become her administrative assistant. Sabrina had joined the company as an entry-level recruiter and had found herself in the entry-level role of HR administrative assistant still five years later when Jeanne transferred her to become her assistant.

As Jeanne's assistant, Sabrina worked diligently to ensure she exceeded expectations. Jeanne knew Sabrina had a degree and experience as a recruiter but became more impressed with her company knowledge, work ethic, and creativity in solving problems. Jeanne asked Sabrina to consider assuming the talent acquisition manager position and she accepted.

Within a month, Sabrina was leading the new function. She designed and implemented the new hiring process, negotiated with vendors for background checks, and then was immediately tasked to staff a new, start-up plant in only ninety days. She completed the task on schedule. The operations VP recognized Sabrina's performance as the start-up plant's new employees reached performance standards well ahead of schedule with nearly no turnover. Jeanne was pleased in how the new manager's knowledge, experience, and skills (human capital) were optimized to achieve unprecedented outcomes.

In the context of a new economy, a changing workplace, and a perceived HR ineffectiveness, a new HR doctrine must be established to provide HR direction in how it functions within itself and for the organization. The doctrine will not be established by improving what HR does but by transforming how HR thinks about itself and how others think about HR. Up to this point in HR's evolution, HR practitioners have worked diligently to improve processes, programs, and systems within the HR field and this served to address administrative and transactional efficiencies. These efforts will continue to be needed. Diligent efforts have also been made to lead organizational change and drive employee engagement, but the focus on the tools and program execution oftentimes overshadows its contributive value in many organizations.

Despite beliefs otherwise, HR's primary effort has been in administering the employment of people. In a conversation with a growing enterprise social software business in Dallas, Texas, its representative explained its need for a new HR leader: "We are looking for someone who has a 'people focus' because, quite honestly, most HR professionals don't have it despite it being their job." On another note, an HR executive was contacted by an out-of-state entrepreneur to consider being the HR leader for his start-up company. The HR executive asked the entrepreneur why he was not searching for local candidates in the large metropolitan area within his state. The entrepreneur stated that the HR professionals in his local area typically knew nothing about business, much less what was needed to start a business. These telling statements are the very essence of HR's predicament: an over-emphasis on administering to people rather than focusing on people and knowing the business. Transforming how HR works requires a new way thinking.

This new thinking will come from a new HR doctrine that will be the catalyst of HR's third transformation. First, this doctrine seeks to have HR truly view an organization's people as a resource—individual by individual—and not as a file or employee number. Past organizational thinking has hindered efforts to view people differently. "Since the Industrial Revolution, the only way a company could scale up in productivity and profit was by treating customers as populations rather than individuals, and by treating employees as positions on an organization chart rather than as unique sources of talent and ideas."[11] Much as other organizational functions optimize their resources to produce or achieve an outcome, this doctrinal approach serves to bring HR into alignment with these functions in a similar purpose and effort. Whereas many HR professionals cite a legal mandate, a process-driven requirement, or a personal standard as justification of their decisions and action, much to the frustration of their peers, the new doctrine presents a renewed focus upon the effective and efficient optimization of people and the human capital they create as a resource to the organization.

Administering employees is necessary for an organization to exist. Optimizing human capital is necessary for an organization to succeed.

Second, the new HR doctrine demands a more closely aligned commitment to the organization's vision and strategy. Whereas HR traditionalists may find this commitment to not be unique, how HR measures its commitment is distinctly different within the new doctrine. It expects HR leaders to monitor the outcomes and impact of people and their human capital against the achievement of the business's strategy and financial objectives. This is a challenging prospect, but an organization's people and their efforts have a direct impact on its success so it must be HR's focus in the optimization of human capital.

Third, the new doctrine places great emphasis on the most important, yet basic interaction that occurs for any business organization—the customer transaction. Actualizing a business organization's vision and strategy singularly narrows to the customer's purchase and repeat purchase of its product or service. Whether it is a retail consumer, parts supplier, or the government, the customer, as a stakeholder, greatly impacts the fortune of all other stakeholders in the organization. The doctrine links an organization's people and people-related programs and systems invariably to the organization's customer. For example, people-related programs that result in employees who are more productive with higher morale and retention are less impactful and somewhat meaningless if the customer is not buying the organization's product or service. This is not a condemnation of such programs but an illustration of how people and people-related programs must be measured in great part by customer behavior as well as by financial impact.

To elaborate further, human capital can be defined as the skills, knowledge, and experience that an individual gains in an organization representing a value or resource to the organization. Optimization is making the best or most effective use of a resource. Therefore, optimizing human capital is ensuring that an organization's people resources generate optimal outcomes to achieve an organization's vision and strategy in satisfying its customers' expectations, needs, and wants.

This doctrinal shift is predicated upon the following assumptions:

- An organization is as successful as the collective success of its individual members in achieving an organizational strategy or goal.
- Each individual in an organization has the potential to measurably contribute to an organization's success.
- People are a resource that must be protected, preserved, and sustained.
- An organization's vision and strategy is synonymous with a beneficent customer relationship; customers drive an organization's focus and effort.

To differentiate this new thinking from past conventional HR thinking, administering employees is necessary for an organization to exist. Optimizing human capital is necessary for an organization to succeed. Ideally, optimizing people is achieved when the "right" person is hired within the "right" environment to create the "right" outcomes. The opening vignette demonstrated this concept in how one individual's talent and the human capital they created was recognized and leveraged to create success despite predispositions that stereotyped her into a limiting role. In an ideal conceptualization, the following model describes how human capital optimization can be actualized.

Figure 1. Human Capital Optimization Actualized

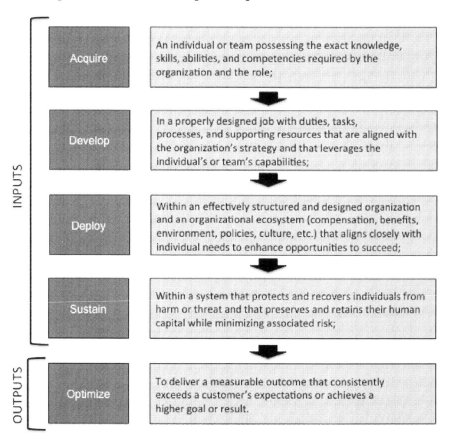

Consequently, HR is able to strive for this idyllic state through the effective design, implementation, and execution of structures, programs, policies, processes, practices, initiatives, and systems that provide an organization's people the greatest opportunity to create optimal outcomes. Thus, HR professionals must become organizational pundits as well as human capital strategists under the new doctrine. Rather than HR's success being measured by its achievement against its own standards and expectations, HR's contribution is measured by how effective an organization's people are in creating the outcomes needed for an organization to succeed.

As previously mentioned, limited research exists that measures the impact of HR on an organization's performance. However, a 2003 study from the *Human Resources Management Journal* did find that progressive HR practices in the areas of selection and staffing, training, performance management, and employee participation within the business units of a large organization did positively impact engagement. This in turn was found to have a positive impact upon operational outcomes, such as workers' compensation cost, productivity, quality, and shrinkage, which further enhanced the business unit's ability to minimize operating expenses and maximize profits.[12] Despite a lack of measurable dollar impact, it can be ascertained that a positive relationship does exist.

Even with its enterprising prospects, the new HR doctrine has its challenges. One challenge is an argument that people cannot be managed as a resource like an inanimate commodity. Whereas raw materials, technology, and equipment can be controlled by human decisions and actions, people are resistant to attempts at complete control and actually respond in a diametric manner. In society, when dictatorial regimes, fundamental religious groups, or autocratic organizations attempt to enforce their will or beliefs upon people, people generally will act subversively to undermine and rebuff that control until an eventual uprising occurs to break from or overturn the ruling group, much as was witnessed across the Middle East in the Arab Spring of 2011. However and in spite of the autonomous nature of individuals, people can still be influenced to make decisions and take action consistent with a direction they might not have otherwise chosen on their own accord. This can be accomplished on the basis of their relationship with the organization and its people, founded upon common values and trust.

Another challenge is that the new doctrine is at risk of being taken out of context with the implication of taking advantage of people. Some may believe that the new doctrine grants permission to selfishly exploit people for the good of the organization. Despite an emphasis on organizational success, an underlying assumption is that organizational success cannot occur without individual successes. And for individuals to be successful, their needs must be satisfactorily met. Those needs may be professional or personal, and HR must work to ensure they are assessed and supported in its goal to optimize people's outcomes and the human capital they create.

Another challenge is that the new doctrine is merely an inversion of the current state of existence. That is to say that the transformational HR specialty areas are being given priority over the transactional specialty areas, as the payroll, compensation, benefits, employee/labor relations, compliance, and legal functions have no apparent or direct bearing on an individual's outcomes. On the contrary, the transactional HR specialty areas serve as a foundation from which to ensure that people as a resource can be optimized. Positive employment transactions and employer–employee relationships have a tremendous bearing on people's confidence and security about their organizations and roles. Rather than a shift in priority of transformational over transactional, the new doctrine sets a purpose and direction for all HR activity.

Finally, HR professionals must also use caution in understanding the difference between optimizing human capital and advocating for employees. As some HR professionals in the new doctrine's course may assume a protector role when it comes to an organization's people, it must be within the broader context of optimizing people as a resource. That is to say that advocacy is a subtext of the greater optimization effort.

Notwithstanding these challenges, getting people to produce the best outcomes within the organizational framework is the essence of optimizing human capital. The new doctrine must be developed in the context of how human beings can achieve their full potential in their organizational role to create a competitive advantage. Much as operations focuses on the product, marketing focuses on the consumer, supply chain focuses on the logistics, and finance focuses on the firm's value, HR must focus on the human capital. People are a resource to the organization and, much as other resources are optimized to get their greatest value, human capital can be optimized by how an organization develops and deploys people to gain the greatest value. This shift in HR thinking is vital to HR's future. In that future, HR will exude more influence and provide a more positive contribution to organizations facing various economic and workplace challenges.

As a doctrine is a declaration of knowledge, ideas, and concepts, it serves primarily to outline rather than to instruct. Therefore, it is to be applied with judgment as it serves as a guide of how to think, not how to do. However, there are key elements that HR professionals should consider in applying the new doctrine that will be described herein as doctrinal principles.

The doctrinal principles involve the development of HR's ethos and praxis. *Ethos* is the psyche that encompasses HR's culture, values, and beliefs. *Praxis* is an accepted practice or method that integrates ethos in its application. These principles support the new HR doctrine and should serve to develop HR professionals for the future.

Chapter Summary

Human capital optimization is a new doctrine for HR professionals. As a guideline, the doctrine presents a renewed people focus, organizational alignment, and customer-driven purpose. Despite challenges to its adoption, HR has the potential to make people a competitive advantage.

1. Does your HR function focus primarily on administering employees or optimizing their contribution?
2. How do you measure HR effectiveness? Does it prioritize organizational alignment or customer impact?

Ethos

Principle #1: Forge HR's Cause

Principle #2: Adopt a Selfless Ethos

Principle #3: Advocate for the Cause

Principle #1:

Forge HR's Cause

"Our job in HR is to protect the company from its employees," stated Richard, VP of employee relations (ER), in a senior HR staff meeting. Robert, the new executive VP of HR, grimaced as he had just joined the large wholesale tool and implement distributor to transform the organization's culture to meet the future business needs of growth and improvement. Richard's words struck a chord with Robert as they represented a direct philosophical conflict about HR's purpose. Robert believed that people were an asset and a strong employer–employee relationship was essential to organizational success. This starkly contrasted with Richard's adversarial position.

Richard had been with the company for five years and had considerable HR experience. Even though some in the meeting gave Richard's comment a tacit nod of approval, others privately warned Robert of Richard's misguided approach that stemmed from an antecedent risk-averse philosophy shared by the legal team and an over-developed ego. Despite the situation's precariousness, Robert was committed to developing Richard and he took time to explain his perspective about employee relations in depth.

As the weeks passed, Richard was often out of sync with Robert's direction as he consistently assumed a confrontational stance with outside counsel and consulting partners and undermined local HR teams by taking employee issues into his own hands. His inability to adapt undermined Robert's efforts to transform HR and the organization's culture. With increasing complaints by the CEO, outside counsel, consultants, and his peers about the VP's decisions and actions, Robert realized Richard was not capable of adapting. He decided to remove Richard from his role and assigned him to a compliance role where he had greater potential to succeed with his skill set.

Robert concluded that he needed to fortify HR's cause with his team and the organization—that enabling employee success was paramount to organizational success.

As defined in this context, a cause is a higher conviction for an ideal purpose that can transcend different organization types, industries, geographies, and sizes. If the cause is just and virtuous, it can give rise to individuals voluntarily choosing to follow it with clarity of purpose and a constant motivating force. Examples of this can be found in the three professions of the military, medicine, and law. Individuals in the US armed forces swear an oath to defend the Constitution from enemies, foreign and domestic. Medical doctors swear to a Hippocratic oath to practice medicine in an ethical and moral manner. Lawyers swear an oath to practice law in a just and fair manner. In each of these fields, individual professionals profess to a higher cause that provides a purpose for their work endeavors.

Such a transcending cause is nonexistent in the discipline of business. Even though many business organizations adopt a code of ethics for their people to follow, these are unique to each organization. As such, the code is not transferable to other business professionals outside the organization as is found instilled devoutly across the military, medical, and legal professions. That does not preclude a business discipline from establishing a cause that creates conviction to a higher purpose to guide the function. Since its inception, HR has lacked a palpable cause and in its void, HR professionals have substituted other motives that ranged from tactical to ideological. As in the opening vignette, an individual or organization may have experience and wisdom but if it is misguided in its cause, it squanders the impact and value of its potential. A lack of purpose leaves individuals and organizations to wander aimlessly in their efforts, resulting more often in failure than success. Thus, to focus HR's effort and expand its vision, HR must define and adopt a cause that transcends the field for a new HR doctrine to take root.

Given its unique role as the only organizational function with people as its principal constituent, HR has the opportunity to find a purpose that centers on people. In support of the human capital optimization doctrine previously discussed, HR's cause is proposed as follows:

Deploy, optimize, and sustain an organization's people and their human capital to achieve organizational success.

Greater than just a focus on people, deploying, optimizing, and sustaining people and their human capital entails a shift of emphasis from the programs, tools, and tasks that administer an organization's employees to an emphasis on what people do, why people do it, and how people can do it best for the most optimal results. This is the essence of HR's new doctrine: a focus on what, why, and how people work in order to influence successful outcomes in support of the organization's vision and strategy in creating successful customer interactions. Whereas in the past HR measured its success on hiring the best talent in the least time, having the fewest payroll errors, or defending against a legal claim, HR's successes must now be measured by the organization's competitive and financial success and by how effective an organization's people are in creating the outcomes to support that success.

An individual or organization may have experience and wisdom, but if it is misguided in its cause, it squanders the impact and value of its potential.

In this, HR's third transformation, the HR field is transformed from a state of function-centrism and myopia to a resource and execution-oriented function. This is predicated on the belief and assumption that every individual that joins an organization has the potential to influence or create outcomes to achieve organizational success. In this new doctrine, each HR professional drives human capital optimization by ensuring that individuals in the organization achieve success in their specific job roles to fulfill the organization's strategy and goals.

As a cause is an ideal, it must be translated into a tangible, workable mission. To do so requires the establishment of a strategic imperative that encapsulates HR's new cause. A strategic imperative is a "must-do" for an organization or function to aspire to and to achieve in pursuit of its cause. The strategic HR imperative that follows from HR's cause is this:

Design and execute programs, policies, processes, practices, and systems to deploy, optimize, and sustain people to achieve optimal outcomes in support of the organization's vision and strategy.

Though this strategic imperative seems benign at first glance, it resets HR's purpose by sparking a shift in how HR executes its work within the function, develops its people, and delivers its services. If HR professionals are asked today if their efforts enable and empower the organization's employees to achieve optimal outcomes, the response would be mixed. Asking HR professionals to enable and empower people to achieve optimal outcomes elevates HR to a highly influential resource that greatly impacts the organization's success. Through the imperative, HR is positioned to more directly help the organization face market challenges, minimize risk, manage its evolution, and enhance the organization's competiveness through its customers.

To reiterate, this new doctrine does not abandon the functional and transactional HR activities but rather leverages their processes, tools, and efficiencies in their execution. It transforms an HR-centric and non-participative mindset that limits the field today in its ability to contribute effectively to the business dialogue. The following example of how HR handles an employee that fails to meet expectations illustrates this mindset shift.

Using conventional thinking, when an employee violates a policy or underperforms, HR investigates the incident, documents the facts, and issues a corrective action. Typically in the form of disciplinary action, this corrective action ensures that the employee is warned that any repeated conduct or performance in this manner may lead to further action including termination of employment. In this way, HR has upheld and enforced a policy and has prepared for a defense should a challenge arise.

Under the new doctrine, when an employee violates a policy or underperforms, HR investigates the incident to discover the underlying causes, considers alternative solutions along with the employee to resolve the root causes, gains a formal agreement from all parties to commit to an identified solution, executes the solution, and monitors progress in an attempt to minimize organizational disruption and reengage an individual's efforts for organizational and individual success. This approach views people as a resource to a greater organizational purpose by finding a path to redemption and getting the individual back on track to better serve that purpose. However, this approach is partially contingent on HR and other business leaders building an organization with people resources that align closely with the organization's purpose, requirements, and culture. Even when errant employees are hired, it should not prevent HR from attempting to get optimal results from an organization's people.

Invariably, keeping people focused on their responsibilities, duties, and tasks without unnecessary distractions is emphasized within the new doctrine. As problems arise for employees in the form of payroll check errors or benefit coverage issues, people must believe that their issues are being given priority and being resolved so as to not detract from their focus and effort to perform their duties. HR professionals must accept that every interaction and opportunity to support an employee heavily influences the optimization dynamic.

This renewed focus potentially rids the field of its sometime adversarial and disengaged reputation and silences critics of HR's lack of strategic contribution. Essentially, the imperative is a reversal of the window through which HR professionals view the world and their role in it. Whereas HR in the past has been reactionary in designing and delivering solutions in response to an event or request, the new imperative requires HR to assume a proactive stance. This entails being purposeful in understanding the organization's processes and technologies and how people can be optimized along with these elements to achieve the organization's business strategy and financial objectives. Just as importantly, HR must view people as a sustainable resource of human capital that must be protected, preserved, and provided for in alignment with a moral, ethical, and legal standard.

With an established cause and strategic imperative, each role in HR has a renewed purpose. The day-to-day activity may not fundamentally change but why and how it is being executed will. All HR professionals have a purpose to ensure that the organization's people are creating optimal outcomes to achieve organizational successes. To do so requires HR professionals to openly subordinate their own agendas for the success of others and the organization.

Principle Summary

HR and most business functions lack a well-defined purpose. A cause defines a common purpose for a profession that transcends organizational boundaries as practiced in the military, law, and medical fields. HR's cause is to optimize an organization's human capital to achieve success. To support it, a strategic imperative to design the HR function to deploy, optimize, and sustain people ensues. By doing so, HR assists organizations to succeed rather than just exist.

1. Does your HR function have a direction or purpose that is well defined?
2. Do your HR or organizational programs regarding people contribute to the organization's success?

Principle #2:

Adopt a Selfless Ethos

The decision was made. Three plants would have to be closed in light of the economic downturn. The CEO knew that the closure of the underperforming plants would impact many families, but it was best for the organization to reduce costs and exposure.

The legal executive suggested to Sarah, the VPHR, that they work quickly to draft the sixty-day Worker Adjustment and Retraining Notification Act (WARN) letter to distribute to employees. Over the course of the next two weeks, the letter was drafted, reviewed, and finally signed. Through HR and outside legal counsel, all employees and the requisite authorities were provided the letter. After announcing its completion during an executive meeting, the legal executive approached Sarah and said, "Well, that's done." She replied quizzically,

"Done? This is just the beginning. We have plants to shutter and employees and their families to out-process."

Sarah knew that the economic downturn would make it difficult for the displaced employees to find new work. In a HR staff meeting, she directed the team to exhaust all possible resources to ensure that the departing employees were well supported in their transition while minimizing the cost impact to the company. This was to be done in addition to their normal workload. This ultimately led to coordinating with state unemployment agencies for onsite, pre- and post-closure assistance, medical and dental plan reviews, the establishment of an employee alumni network, and job reassignment and relocation considerations and actions. Sarah even made personal visits to each plant to check in with employees and ask what more could be done to help with their transition. Employees were then honored with a plant luncheon on their final day.

In the end, an employee sent a message to Sarah: "I was laid off before by another company, but they never cared about us as much as this company did. Thank you."

Some HR professionals are inclined to take a function-centric perspective that has the potential to manifest into a sense of self-importance. This perspective can further lead to behaviors that are not conducive to serving the organization's vision and strategy. Nonetheless, there are some HR professionals that adopt customer-service principles in serving an organization's employees. But even these individuals sometimes miss extending these principles beyond the one-to-one interactions to serve the organization's broader needs. As the new HR doctrine is predicated upon serving the organization's interests, it requires a climate in which the success of others and the organization is at the forefront of each individual HR professional's activity. Such a climate must be derived from a culture that elevates an organization's people and their human capital so that it is leveraged for success. This concept is enshrined in the army leadership value of selfless service. In the army, selfless service is defined as "putting the welfare of the nation, the army, and subordinates before your own."[13]

For a nonmilitary organization, selfless service is a critical cultural element that promotes the organization and individual's success above one's self-interest. Selfless service offers a purity of purpose, uninfluenced by a personal agenda, that gives rise to clarity of effort. The clarity of purpose resulting from a selfless character enables leaders and employees to execute an organization's vision, mission, and strategy effectively through its people, processes, and technologies.

Being selfless also requires an ethical, moral, and legal basis that pervades an individual and organization's decision making, behaviors, and actions. In the words of famous American humorist Mark Twain, "Always do right. This will gratify some people, and astonish the rest." By being selfless in performing their work, some will come to appreciate and recognize these leaders for their uncommon character. Before adopting a servant or service leadership approach, or before a leader can become an inspiration to others, a leader must internalize the trait of selfless service. By internalizing this leadership quality, the HR leader or professional is able to circumnavigate most political obstacles by putting the interest of the greater organization first.

Selfless service offers a purity in purpose uninfluenced by a personal agenda that gives rise to clarity of effort.

To internalize the selfless service trait, special emphasis must be placed upon six critical attributes that can be further developed. These attributes are benevolence, humility, clemency, gratitude, civility, and empathy. They may appear on the surface as "soft," but they serve as cornerstone principles for great achievements. Many great historical figures leveraged these attributes to overcome adversity and accomplish great things. Notable leaders such as Revolutionary War hero and first American president George Washington, Civil War leaders Abraham Lincoln and Joshua Chamberlain, and Indian nationalist leader Mahatma Gandhi led their lives with a selfless service trait. By developing the attributes that fortify this trait, HR professionals can experience their best moments in serving others.

Benevolence

Noun: well-meaning, desire to do good to others

In colonial India, Mahatma Gandhi was faced with overwhelming adversity in his attempts to secure Indian independence from Great Britain. Despite mistreatment and imprisonment throughout his life at the hands of the British, Gandhi promoted the tactic of nonviolence toward achieving his goals. Heavily influenced by religious and philosophical teachings, Gandhi saw violence against another human being as deplorable. Despite threats, assassination attempts, and political pressure to step aside, Gandhi courageously held to his principle of ensuring that resistance to the British crown was done through nonviolent means. His efforts to unite religious factions into a single nation, elevate women's position in Indian society, and gain independence from Britain were absent of selfish ambition; he worked with a selfless drive to prevent harm to his people and his adversaries.[14]

Decisions and actions based on a well-meaning, just, and fair intent are a foundational underpinning to selfless service in the workplace. This is counter to the self-interest and self-indulgence common to the many leaders and individuals who directly contributed to the underlying causes of the Great Recession. HR leaders mired in an HR-centric approach may perceive their decisions and actions as well meaning but may actually miss the broader needs of the organization and its people.

Seldom will leaders face the adversity or pressure that was exacted upon Gandhi; however, many leaders will regularly face the opportunity to perform selflessly with good intentions. Approaching responsibilities, duties, and tasks with the intention to serve the organization and its people is empowering for leaders as it frees them from political entanglements that stem from power, status, and control. However, peer pressure and self-interests will inevitably arise. Despite it being easier to say than to do, leaders must recognize these unfavorable influences and remain focused on performing their duties for the good of the organization and its people in a just, fair, and benevolent manner. Benevolent leaders who are just in their methods and approach are recognized as reliable and trustworthy and can later be relied upon as a resource for success.

Humility

Noun: a modest view of one's own importance

Before becoming the United States' first president, George Washington was at the peak of his popularity having led the Revolutionary Army to victory over Great Britain, the world's greatest global power of the era. As the founding fathers met to draft the new government's structure, the discussion expectedly came to the question of who the new nation's leader would be. Washington knew he was a highly recognized, respected, and influential individual given his battlefield successes and could have easily used his influence for personal gain by seizing power. Moreover, many people wanted Washington to assume the new country's leadership role and to bestow upon him a title common to European heads of state. Washington had enormous support and could have easily assumed control of the fledging nation if his personal interests and ego had led him to do so.

But his actions spoke volumes about his restrained sense of self-importance. He resigned as general of the Continental Army immediately after peace was negotiated, although he was in an opportune position to use his power and the army's resources to act on selfish ambition. He made no attempt to seize power but did not shun the opportunity to lead the nation when his compatriots asked him to do so. Upon being elected president, he asked to be addressed only as chief executive when others suggested the titles of royalty. He also set precedent in limiting his presidency to two terms, demonstrating his commitment to the democratic principles that were being forged in the new nation and the conviction that no one person should be above that cause.[15] By subduing his self-importance and subordinating his personal interest for the best interests of the nation, President Washington's acts of humility suppressed the temptation of power and riches that allowed the nation to evolve as a democracy.

True humility is often hard to come by as most individuals have a need or a desire to be relevant. In their path to relevance, individuals are driven to work hard to achieve goals and objectives as they progress through their career and achieve success. Having confidence and strong self-esteem provides individuals with the mindset needed to overcome adversity and uncertainty. With each success comes greater confidence and stronger self-esteem. Growing success and feelings of self-importance can lead to a path of either humility or arrogance.

Unfortunately, some leaders, whether emerging leaders or seasoned C-level leaders, choose to place their ambition, personal status, and position above the organization and others. This leadership arrogance and self-centeredness undermines the leader. Arrogant leaders provide a fragile commitment level and dubious support, creating a tenuous structure that further detracts from the organization's strategy and mission. In substituting self-interest or any other purpose or agenda above the organization's purpose, the leader is exposed as misaligned with the organization. This allows for less-than-acceptable bargaining and compromises that promote these self-interests and further detract from the organization's strategy.

But other leaders are able to be conscious of their path to success. They acknowledge their personal role as well as the roles of others and the events that contributed to their success. They are also able to keep their organization's greater purpose and the success of its people toward achieving that purpose in the forefront of their efforts. Through humility, a leader has a clear conscience and can work selflessly toward achieving the organization's strategy and purpose, much as Washington was able to do as the United States' first president.

Clemency

Noun: forgiveness

As the Civil War was nearing its end, some Northerners, historically known as Radical Republicans, believed that the South should be punished for their actions in seceding from the union and even more so for their immoral support of slavery. The proposed punishments ranged from denying Southerners their voting rights to preventing some from continuing in their chosen professions in law and education. President Abraham Lincoln understood that the great cause of preserving the union and ensuring the equality of all people by freeing the slaves would be greatly undermined by such acts of vengeance and retaliation. He supported a stance of reunifying the South with the union by granting amnesty to Southerners and moving the country much more quickly on a path of reconciliation and reconstruction. In his second inaugural speech, Lincoln's famous words "with malice toward none, with charity for all" demonstrated his vision of forgiving past transgressions and focusing the nation on a future of reunification rather than dwelling on the past through punishment.[16] Unfortunately, he did not survive to enact his vision, but his opinions influenced the reconstruction debate in the years following the Civil War.

Many emerging and developed leaders fall into the trap of a right-and-wrong or black-and-white approach to issues, particularly when they involve people. In their attempt to uphold what they believe to be correct, these leaders can become vindictive and vengeful in the handling of employee errors, mistakes, or wrongful actions. This sometimes occurs with HR professionals. As previously cited, the effort to investigate and punish employees becomes the objective. Lincoln faced a similar confrontation in that some Northerners became focused on the South's punishment rather than the greater purpose of reunifying the nation.

Forgiveness can be described as a selfish act of liberation. Through forgiveness, individuals can unburden themselves from anger and vengeance so that they can move forward without emotional strain. In this way, the individual has a clear conscience that affords him or her the opportunity to focus on a greater purpose. By adopting the principle of clemency, a leader can selflessly face transgressions objectively to move quickly through reconciliation and to the recovery of trust.

In a practical illustration, a leader with a clear focus on the organization's purpose can objectively investigate a transgression or shortcoming to determine the underlying causes. Once identified, the leader can work with the transgressor to eliminate the causes of the problem; this may include either behavioral or environmental changes. By providing an opportunity for the individual to participate and correct the behavior or performance rather than unilaterally exacting a punishment, a leader essentially reframes the transgression. The focus shifts from exacting vengeance to resolving issues and thus remains focused on the organizational strategy and vision. The process is predicated upon selflessly forgiving the transgression and moving forward.

By doing so, the organization is minimally disrupted as the transgressor is provided a second chance and the organization retains and avoids the costs of a disgruntled individual or a replacement employee. As a caveat, being forgiving does not suggest that people not be held accountable for misdeeds. It merely suggests that the focus is selflessly on what is best for the organization and the individual and that may be realized in a parting of ways in some instances.

Gratitude

Noun: the quality of being thankful; readiness to show appreciation

Leaders, and many other people, too often become focused on the demands of the day and move from conversation to conversation or activity to activity in a seamless transition to be as efficient with their time as possible. In their efforts, they encounter many individuals who are also just as intently tending to the tasks that fill their day. However, a 2012 survey by the John Templeton Foundation, a nonprofit organization that sponsors research on creativity, gratitude, freedom, and other related topics, reported that only 10 percent of adults say thank you to a colleague each day and only 7 percent express gratitude to their boss.[17] We often don't pause to be thankful for the contribution that an individual is making for the organization unless it's at a special event. Many people are appreciative of someone else's efforts when that effort yields a personal favor or encouragement but never think to show appreciation for an individual's efforts to a purpose or cause.

Gratitude for an individual's efforts reinforces and encourages the commitment, behaviors, and decisions that are being made to achieve the organizational strategy. For individuals, organizational leaders embody its strategy and purpose and the gratitude they convey represents a selfless acknowledgment of the organization's success through the contributions of its people.

Civility

Noun: courtesy in behavior or speech

Reality television's growing popularity pervades American culture. Some of these programs engender a mood of incivility across a broad swath of the population. These select reality TV programs' mantra seems to be to argue disagreeably, challenge disrespectfully, and mock others at their expense. Each week, flocks of viewers tune in to their favorite reality TV program to be entertained by individuals who appear as egocentric, disagreeable, disrespectful, selfish, and spiteful. Many people have noticed a growing disrespect in social situations. Road rage in rush-hour traffic and poor customer service experiences are indicators that people view others in a disrespectful manner. Concurrently, the Internet empowers individuals, cloaked behind cyber anonymity, to ridicule, condemn, and harass others with a noticeable absence of social grace.

Considering the close quarters and frequent interactions of a large workforce, civility in the workplace is more important now than ever before. A necessary balance is jeopardized by this growing trend that undermines an organization's productivity, morale, and effectiveness in the workplace. In extreme cases, an uncivil exchange can create workplace issues that result in distrust and in worst cases, violence. The emotional fallout from an unpleasant exchange is distracting and makes it more difficult for people to perform at their best.

Civility allows for the open and honest discussion necessary to resolve issues. By promoting civility in their actions and behaviors, HR professionals can help to deescalate the emotions of these matters to remain focused on the desired outcomes. Civility is the lubricant that enables society, organizations, and people to overcome the friction of differences in order to cooperate or compromise in finding a solution. Its absence is a risk and liability that may generate organizational disruption and create unaccountable cost in both the short and long term. The lack of civility witnessed in the US Congress since 2010 essentially has

76

rendered it ineffective and incapable of resolving national issues with a notable absence of compromise and progress. Invariably, the underlying goal for any organization is for individuals to conduct themselves selflessly and, conversely, to be treated with respect. By restraining their egos and self-interest, individuals can be civil in all matters, even while disagreeing, to accomplish a goal.

Empathy

Noun: the ability to understand and share the feelings of others

When General Ulysses S. Grant accepted the surrender of Confederate forces from General Robert E. Lee at Appomattox Court House, he sent Brigadier General Joshua Lawrence Chamberlain, esteemed for his role in the Battle of Gettysburg, to lead the formal ceremony of the Confederate Army's surrender the next day. At the ceremony, the defeated Confederate units were to march past the Union Army and then stack their arms as a condition of their surrender. As the ceremony began, Chamberlain was so moved by the beleaguered and half-starved Confederate soldiers that assembled before him into orderly units and then began their deliberate march past him with an unusual discipline and pride despite the humiliation of their defeat that he immediately ordered his soldiers to attention and then to present arms to salute each passing unit. Chamberlain did this not as a salute to the Confederate cause but to honor and welcome his compatriots' return to the Union, despite the possibility of this gesture being viewed negatively by many Northerners. In response to the Union soldiers' act, the Confederate officers ordered their units to return the salute as they passed. Many viewed Chamberlain's empathetic gesture of rendering respect and upholding the dignity of a fallen adversary as the beginning of the nation's healing.[18]

Individuals who can empathize with the plight of others possess an innate gift of perspective. Perspective is an advantage that enables better understanding and appreciation of the circumstances and issues that arise in relationships. It is truly a needed advantage for the HR professional, who often deals with employees in their most vulnerable or exalted moments. Empathy is in itself a selfless ability to share the burden or joy of others and then assess and determine what is needed or desired to create optimal outcomes.

Colonel Chamberlain's empathy for his defeated enemy demonstrates how, as a combatant, he was able to fight his enemy for the cause of freeing slaves and reunifying the nation, yet he was human enough to understand the emotion and sacrifice endured by his adversaries. Of all the roles in an organization, the HR professional must assume an objective stance in ensuring an organization's mission and HR's cause are fulfilled, yet be human enough to empathize with individuals who experience difficulties in their role, in their relationships, or in their personal lives. Similar to the view taken by Chamberlain's contemporaries, HR professionals have the opportunity to resolve issues involving people in order to progress with the broader organization's vision and purpose.

A selfless ethos repositions the HR professional's perspective from an inward to an outward viewpoint that underscores the new HR doctrine. By adopting a selfless motive, HR professionals fulfill the expectations of organizational peers by focusing on the organization's success. By adopting a selfless service trait emboldened with the critical attributes of benevolence, humility, clemency, gratitude, civility, and empathy, the HR professional personifies trustworthiness and virtuousness that establishes credibility with key constituents—the organization and its people.

Principle Summary

HR professionals are being challenged to devote themselves to a cause that serves the organization through the optimization of human capital. Doing so requires a selfless service approach to support an organization and its workforce. Benevolence, humility, clemency, gratitude, civility, and empathy are important attributes in transforming the HR professional's ethos. With a selfless service ethos, HR professionals gain an outward perspective about their role and impact.

1. Do you find your HR team making decisions from a function-centric or organization-centric basis?
2. Serving the organization can be interpreted in many ways. How does your HR team interpret serving the organization?

Principle #3:

Advocate for the Cause

Two HR professionals approached Ellen, their HR leader, about an employee issue and their plan to address it. The situation involved an employee who had a family coverage benefit plan and whose child had exceeded the eligibility coverage age, rendering the employee with a less expensive employee plus spouse plan. The employee was contacted by the insurance carrier to inform him of the change and that all would be properly handled. Nearly a year passed before the employee realized that the company was still making deductions from his paycheck for the higher coverage level. He asked the HR department for assistance in updating his coverage and retrieving his over-contributed funds estimated at $1,500.

The two HR professionals' solution was to repay the employee only half of the money as punishment, explaining that he should have reviewed his paychecks and alerted HR sooner with the problem. Ellen asked about the employee and learned he had more than fifteen years of excellent service. She asked them if the deduction overages negatively impacted the company, if the money was inaccessible, and if any rule or regulation prevented repayment. To all, the answer was no. Ellen then asked if the insurance carrier had notified the company of the change along with the employee at the time of the coverage change. The answer was no.

Ellen challenged the pair to consider the alternatives. The company could advocate for a good employee by repaying him all "his" money or it could keep half of it with no right to do so and possibly disengage the employee and negatively impact the business. Ellen asked the two HR professionals to repay the employee his money and fix the process to avoid a repeat error.

The two individuals gave Ellen a puzzled glance. "But it's not our fault," they said. "He should be held accountable for not reviewing his paystubs, not us (HR)."

In the new doctrine, emerging HR leaders and professionals are asked to assume a proactive role in seeking out opportunities within their influence or control to optimize the organization's people and the human capital they create in support of the organization's vision and strategy. In the natural course of organizations, conflicts will arise between two or more people or two or more viewpoints. In the opinion of many, conflict is not always an undesirable thing. Reasonable conflict forces a comparison of reasoning that strengthens an idea or position. Inevitably, sometimes parties are unable to resolve a conflict and they require a third party to provide a fair and objective solution to the issue. This is the role of the mediator.

In contrast, an advocate is an individual who supports a cause or is a representative on behalf of another individual. The latter representative definition has been HR's label as employee advocates. But it is the former definition of advocating for a cause that best aligns HR professionals to their more practical role as mediators. HR professionals must advocate for optimizing human capital to achieve organizational success in their attempts to mediate conflict between stakeholders.

In the opening vignette, the HR professionals failed to evaluate the impact of their recommendation. As they advocated solely for HR's interest with minimal regard for the individual, the transactional "tit for tat" mindset failed to seize the opportunity to build functional credibility and employee loyalty. These individuals could not envision the possibility that their recommendation could work counter to the organization's best interests, resulting in a lose–lose scenario. If carried out, the HR department possibly would have been perceived as unsympathetic, causing the employee to become disgruntled and possibly unmotivated to perform after being denied repayment of the money he'd earned. Collateral damage from the employee potentially informing his peers could have further harmed HR's and the organization's credibility with its employees for the paltry sum of $750.

On the other hand, and at no cost to the company, the HR professionals could have taken advantage of a simple opportunity to promote HR, the organization, and build positive relationships. By repaying the employee all his money in a prompt manner, the employee may have thought no differently about the company, as he believed the money was his in the first place. However, the chance to build HR's credibility and position the company's reputation as a benevolent employer was presented by the situation. Through the interaction, the HR professionals could have also positively reinforced the employee's work record and linked the repayment of his money as an act of appreciation for his effort. Across the board, an opportunity was missed to advocate in a broader sense.

This scenario demonstrates that HR professionals at times advocate on behalf of a detached motive. They sometimes assume that preserving the process or holding people accountable are the most important factors in their decision making. If an employee fails to follow a well-established process, the employee is perceived as a problem, undeserving of consideration, and the recommended actions to resolve the issue neglect what might be best for the organization.

Advocating on an employee's behalf or to uphold a policy or process does not necessarily yield the most organizational benefit. Independently, each is narrow in its reach and disenfranchised in its impact. Realistically, advocacy and mediation are not simple tasks, particularly in an organization of diverse functions and multitudes of individual personalities. Within an organization, the complexity of interests is exponential. In a somewhat cynical yet pragmatic manner, here are some possible varying interests of key stakeholders in any organization:

- Shareholders want the highest return for their investment through management's optimization of assets and resources.[19]
- Customers or clients want products or services with the best value and the best features for the lowest price.
- Companies or suppliers want the highest price for the least cost in selling its products and services.
- Companies want the most out of its resources (people) for the lowest cost in creating its products and services.

- Individuals want the highest worth for their work for the least sacrifice in creating products and services.[20]

These interests should not be viewed in a negative or selfish light. But if the core motives of each group were minimalized, these interests may be relatively close to what each stakeholder would pursue. At a glance, each of these positions has a natural conflict with another. Within these conflicting positions, the most challenging may be between shareholder and individuals (as management), customer and company, and company and individuals. Issues most often arise when it is perceived that the interests of one party are repudiated for the interests of another party.

HR professionals must advocate for optimizing human capital to achieve organizational success in their attempts to mediate conflict between stakeholders.

HR professionals must understand the motives of key stakeholders while appreciating the organization's vision, mission, and goals, and executing upon the strategic HR imperative. As the new doctrine is embodied in optimizing human capital to create optimal outcomes for the organization to succeed, HR professionals have this as their cause to advocate. For the most part, this advocacy approach transcends the varying stakeholder interests. Advocating for positions or for remedies that support organizational success above the individual interests of an executive, a manager, a customer, a shareholder, or an employee is the ideal approach. However, by choosing this advocacy approach, the best outcome ultimately may be in support of a key stakeholder's position given the situation and circumstances. Albeit vague and open to interpretation, the best outcome in this context is that position or remedy that achieves the best advantage for the greater organization's vision and strategy with the least risk or loss.

In their role as advocates and mediators, HR professionals must avoid the belief that they hold the foremost viewpoint. HR professionals are just as fallible as any other individual and may not always have all the necessary facts to reach the best conclusion. This is not to imply that an HR professional's judgment or perspective is incorrect in comparison with the judgment or perspective of others, but rather that the HR professional's viewpoint must always be pointed for the organization's good while being open to all perspectives.

Such an advocacy and mediation requires wisdom and judgment in interpretation and application. HR professionals must learn not to insert themselves as antagonists into a situation or circumstance, but rather assume a protagonist position to view all angles and sides of a situation objectively. In approaching a situation or circumstance, an effective advocate and mediator must research and gain an understanding of the issues:

- Who are the parties involved? Keep in mind that not all parties may have knowledge of the situation and may not have a voice—their position must still be represented by a party representative or the advocate.
- Determine the facts of the situation to facilitate moving past blaming to resolution.
  - What event or action transpired?
  - Who was the catalyst of the event or action?
  - What was the underlying cause(s)?
  - What were the consequences and their impact to all parties?
- What are the conflicting positions? Consider other parties that are impacted but that may not have an active involvement or participation.
- What is the remedy sought by each party and what are the consequences?
- How does the remedy measure up with regard to achieving the organization's strategy, goals, and financial objectives, the strategic HR imperative, and the best outcome? This remedy may

or may not be represented by the parties and may require the advocate to develop.

- How does the remedy measure up with a moral, legal, and ethical standard?
- Advocate for the remedy that most adequately supports the organization's strategy, goals, and objectives within a moral, legal, and ethical framework that minimizes risk or loss.

Advocating for the organization's success mitigates the solitary and conventional employee advocacy approach and minimizes the narrow policy and/or process-driven advocacy by encompassing a broader view. Be aware that advocating is not an extreme "take no prisoners" support of a position unless extraordinary moral, legal, or ethical implications exist. In this doctrine, advocating is searching for a remedy with the best possible outcome for the organization. As difficult as it may be to foresee in this discussion, advocating for the organization's success may be perceived as picking sides as in one matter it may appear HR is advocating for an employee's position whereas in another matter it may appear HR is advocating for the organization. Regardless of appearances, the HR professional must maintain a professional objectivity with a fair and consistent judgment. Being a just and fair advocate and mediator gives HR professionals credibility in that HR is not about taking sides but about representing the success of the organization and the individual for the immediate and long term.

Principle Summary

HR's role as an advocate is divided. On one hand, HR advocates for the employee as promoted, and on the other hand, HR advocates for the organization as practiced. Advocacy is defined as either supporting a cause or representing an individual. It is the former definition that best defines HR's role within the new doctrine. In a more practical sense, HR mediates conflict between stakeholders while advocating for HR's cause.

1. Is your HR function at times conflicted between advocating for employees and for the organization?
2. How does your HR team's advocacy role impact its trust and effectiveness with your organization and with its employees?

Praxis

Principle #4: Be an Organizational Pundit

Principle #5: Deliver HR on the Organization's Terms

Principle #6: Design HR with the Organization's Customer in Mind

6.1: Deploy People with a Superior Advantage

6.2: Optimize People as an Asset

6.3: Sustain People as a Resource

Principle #4:

Be an Organizational Pundit

Phil, a manager, was searching for a strong candidate for a very critical role. He worked hard to attract and source the best candidates possible. Finally, a candidate had been identified after completing the selection process. An offer was extended to the candidate. In the negotiation process, the candidate asked Phil for the organization's benefit plan coverage levels and premium information. Phil passed on the request to Michael, the HR leader, who instructed his benefits director to provide the candidate with the information.

A week later Michael followed up with Phil to check on the candidate's status. Phil said that he had spoken to the candidate who was still waiting for the benefits information to make a final decision.

Michael then went to the benefits director and asked him if he had sent the information to the candidate as directed. The director said no. Michael asked him why. The director explained that the candidate was not an employee and until he became employed he would not be privy to the company's confidential information.

Michael then informed the director of how the candidate's expertise could assist the organization in recouping nearly a million dollars in losses from faulty claim management. As a discussion point, he asked the director to consider a risk (cost)/benefit analysis of sharing the benefit information with the candidate and to explain his business decision.

The director replied with agitation, "He is not an employee and if he wants the benefits information so badly, then he should accept the offer." Michael realized his director could not appreciate the circumstances much less assess the situation from a business or organizational perspective. Moments later, the candidate called to decline the offer. He had accepted another company's offer.

As previously discussed, HR has its roots in administrative and transactional duties and tasks. However, as HR professionals progress in their careers, new challenges arise that demand a broader knowledge base. As in many other pursuits, the knowledge, skills, and abilities that may have created success in one role at one level may not be the same that are needed in a different role or at a different level. As in the opening vignette, HR professionals can become the victims of their limited expertise and, in extreme cases, when these individuals are faced with their limitations, it can be difficult to overcome, creating a burden on the organization.

The new economy and its challenges will require emerging HR leaders and professionals to possess greater knowledge about the organizations they support. As previously mentioned, HR professionals and academics have worked diligently to develop the HR skill and competency model that enabled HR to be highly effective in the transactional and functional areas of the HR field. However, to be highly effective in serving the organization beyond HR's dominion and to enable better outcomes from people, emerging HR leaders and professionals must appreciate the organizational functions and the business context within which they conduct their duties and responsibilities. HR leaders should then be expected to strategically position the HR function within this context to satisfy organizational strategy and goals with this expanded expertise.

Understanding the underlying business concepts enables the HR leader to engage in meaningful business collaboration with an organization's strategies, processes, systems, and stakeholders.

This expertise must include an understanding of general business concepts, the variables that influence an organization's ability to compete, and the strategy and direction employed by an organization to achieve success. Understanding the underlying business concepts enables the HR leader to engage in meaningful business collaboration within an organization's strategies, processes, systems, and stakeholders. To gain this much-needed knowledge, HR professionals must seek out avenues to attain it. Many colleges and universities offer professional certificates in business that provide HR professionals a less resource-intensive path to gaining a business understanding. Ideally, enrolling in a university for a full degree in business yields the best opportunity to gain this knowledge. HR professionals may also seek out and ask business peers to educate them on their specific business discipline as they progress through their career. HR professionals must know that in HR's nonleadership roles *developing* business acumen is beneficial and that in HR's leadership roles *possessing* business acumen is essential.

By possessing business expertise, HR professionals are in a position to better understand how an organization functions, specifically with regard to its people and their human capital. HR leaders can then better negotiate and contribute in discussions regarding each business function and its people. Whereas developing a formal business expertise is beyond the realm of this book, it is within the scope of the next few paragraphs to present the general concepts, influencing variables, and strategic direction that drive an organization's existence.

Business Concepts

Knowing Why a Customer Buys an Organization's Products/Services

Simply, the existence and success of an organization is contingent upon a customer purchasing its products or services in a broad marketplace. HR professionals must clearly understand their organization's product or service offering and the market being served. The product or service offering typically provides unique features and benefits for its customer portfolio that differentiates it from its market competitors. Ultimately, customers make their buying decision based on a value proposition that fulfills their need or want. That is, the customer realizes value in the product/service's designed features and its derived benefits. Being knowledgeable in this value proposition is essential for an HR professional to understand the product/service attributes that an organization's people create in their work that satisfies a customer's needs and wants.

However, customers do not always purchase an organization's products or services without some persuasion. Organizations, through their marketing efforts, must persuade customers to purchase their products or services. To do so, marketers must deliberately answer a need or create a desire within the customer to own the product or to subscribe to the service ahead of alternative providers or substitute products or services. The features, attributes, and benefits are encapsulated in a brand that symbolizes the value of the products and services. The value of the brand grows with the consistency and reliability of an organization's products and services and through the persistent advertising and messaging to communicate the value proposition to the customer.

A much more involved effort is made in positioning the product or service in a competitive market to attract the greatest number of customers, or market share. The HR professional must become knowledgeable about the organization's relative existence in that market. Organizational size, scope, structure, market position, and reputation are important to know.

- Is the organization a market leader or a follower?
- Is it an innovator or cost leader?
- What are the organization's reliable and established products/ services within established markets and what are the organization's new products/services and emerging markets?

Through the CEO or business unit leader, the HR leader should learn how the market has evolved and how the organization's clients, customers, and competitors are adapting to these shifts in the marketplace.[21] In that vein, HR professionals must gain an understanding of the market's size, its maturity and development, and the chief competitors.

- Is the market large or small?
- Is the market growing or shrinking?
- Are there emerging markets?
- Who are the most threatening competitors and why?
- What is known about the competitors relative to size, scope, structure, market position, and reputation?

Also, HR professionals can learn from the marketing team how customers view and adopt the organization's products or services in the marketplace. The Boston Consulting Group created the Boston Matrix in an attempt to define a product or service position relative to the competitive market. Essentially, it provides organizations an insight if certain organizational conditions exist in the markets within which its products or services compete.[22]

Figure 1. Boston Matrix: Product or Service Profile

Boston Matrix	High Market Share	Low Market Share
Growing Markets	Rising Star	Problem Child
Mature Markets	Cash Cow	Dog

In most cases, an organization wants its product or service to be a "rising star" or a "cash cow." This means that its product or service has a dominating market share in a growing or fully developed market with few competitors or innovations. But even these are not secure positions as consumer habits change over time or new competitors enter the market. By understanding how an organization's product or service is situated in the competitive market, a CEO and staff adjust the organization's strategy or refine the product or service offering to move it to a more favorable position. HR professionals need to be fully aware of this evolving dynamic as the demands on an organization's people may be varied from new marketing approaches, to product innovation, to reduced costs.

To assist the CEO and staff in forming a new strategy, the Ansoff Product-Market Matrix presents marketing strategies based on the existence or creation of markets or of products and services. That is, given a specific market condition, an organization may shift its product and/or service marketing approach to create demand where it does not exist to gain market share.[23]

Figure 2. Ansoff Product-Market Matrix

Ansoff Product-Market Matrix	Existing Products	New Products
Existing Markets	Market Penetration	Product Development
New Markets	Market Development	Diversification

For example, a can of chicken noodle soup is an existing product. In the existing soup market niche of the consumer foods industry, an organization must attempt to *penetrate* the market with recipe or product enhancements, advertisement, or promotion of its soup to gain greater interest, acceptance, and ultimately market share. If all of a sudden some soups are found to have medicinal attributes, a potential new market is created for its soups and the organization may attempt to *develop* the new market of eating chicken noodle soup as a soothing concoction for colds or flus. The organization may decide to replace the noodle in its soup recipe with a different pasta as a new product. Here, the organization must build an awareness about the product in the existing soup market to *develop* its acceptance. Finally, the organization *diversifies* its product by putting its soup into innovative microwaveable lunch cups that can be used for school or work lunches outside the home and markets to the unique consumer who sees a value in the concept.

Becoming informed about major market trends, how competitors are responding, and how customers are driving changes could have tremendous implications as to how the organization performs currently and into the future. Whereas the impact of a shifting marketing strategy may be minimal to the HR professional's transactional duties, the strategy has the potential to influence the culture and commitment of the organization's people, hence their contribution. This analysis provides the HR professional perspective on the demands and needs of the organization and how people may contribute as a resource.

Knowing How an Organization Produces and Delivers Its Products/Services

An organization must be capable of producing and delivering its products or services in a consistent, effective, and efficient manner to win and retain the customer's confidence and use of the same. Organizations do so through distinct business functions. Combined, these functions create a value chain.

Michael Porter, a business strategist, first introduced the value-chain concept in his book *Competitive Strategy: Techniques for Analyzing Industries and Competitors* in 1980. The concept offered a graphical representation of how a for-profit organization operates. The value chain consists of the primary activities of inbound logistics, operations, outbound logistics, marketing and sales, and service. In support of these core efforts, a firm's infrastructure (legal, finance, accounting, quality), human resources, information technology, and procurement comprise the support activities.[24] Ideally, all activities work in concert to generate organizational value.

98

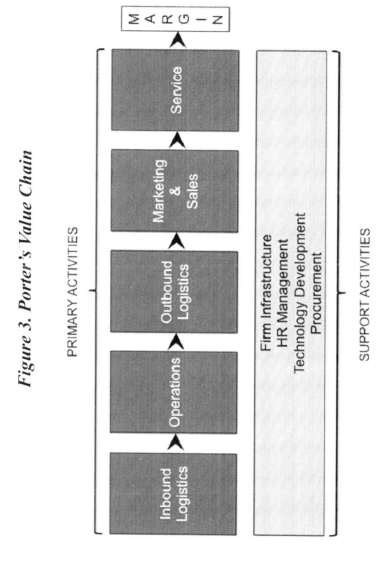

Figure 3. Porter's Value Chain

99

HR professionals should become familiar with each activity and the functions that support the organization. To be in the best position to provide support and advice, an HR professional must have a comprehensive knowledge of how each activity operates within the value chain of the organization.

Whereas marketing is important in persuading customers to buy an organization's products or services, sales is critical in negotiating and closing the purchase transaction. Generating revenue is by far the most important activity of any for-profit organization. The appropriate mix of price and value for the organization's product and service in relation to competing suppliers and products is the negotiating tool used by a sales team to win the customer's purchase decision. Without revenue derived from a sale, the organization is unable to generate the cash flow necessary to produce its products or services, to pay its loan interests, its taxes, and the depreciation or amortization of its assets, nor to earn a profit. By virtue of this reality, the sales force is under the most scrutiny with the highest expectation of any role in an organization and therefore much effort goes into acquiring, developing, and retaining effective sales talent.

An organization's operations and supply chain (inbound and outbound logistics) departments are important in fulfilling the customer's need or want after the sale has been made. This is done through the procurement, processing, production, service, inventory, and distribution of products or services. By design, both operations and supply chain are cost drivers and constantly search for methods to be most efficient with tools, equipment, resources, and processes available. However, the reliability and consistency of a product or service's quality is the most important contribution to be made by the operations and supply chain effort. Without quality, the ability to gain a customer's confidence and purchase decision is greatly at risk. As the organization's operations and supply chain typically utilize the greatest amount of people resources, a high volume of HR support and guidance is typically required to assist them in their efforts to be efficient and reliable in their outputs.

Service is also a critical function as this is a primary channel of communication between a customer and the organization. In one way, customers can contact the organization to purchase a product or use a service that customarily generates a sale. In another way, customers most often contact an organization when their need or expectations are unfulfilled by the organization's products or services. In either situation, how the organization interacts with the customer is critical to continuing the relationship with that customer or more directly, whether that customer will buy again.

Within each of these organizational functions, people are needed to fulfill the customer's expectations. HR professionals have an opportunity to influence how people fulfill these expectations by how HR engages with these functions to optimize its people.

Knowing How an Organization Is Rewarded for Selling, Delivering, and Producing Its Products and Services

Organizations are in business for the reward of profit. As presented, that profit is derived from revenue gained from sales to customers minus the organization's cost or financial obligations to generate that revenue and to operate the organization. This profit translates into rewards for key stakeholders. As shareholders are the owners of the organization, their primary interest is in ensuring that what they own—the organization's assets—are being properly maintained and utilized to create a tangible and intangible value for the assets, their reward.[25] Employees' primary interest is to continue to be secure in their employment and their reward is comprised of compensation and benefits.

The organization's financial objectives augment the organization's strategy to create value. HR professionals must understand that the objectives on a base level typically reflect a revenue target, an earnings objective, or a profit goal. An organization's operational efforts and people's contributions are primarily reflected in the organization's financial statements. Thus, HR professionals must not only learn to create a departmental budget and track department spending, but they must also become familiar with the organization's financial statements. Specifically, the income statement is important to learn as it is a financial view of an organization's revenue from products and services sold and the costs related to producing and selling the products and services. In senior leadership meetings, leaders often discuss efforts to affect the top line and bottom line of the organization.

As *top line* refers to gross sales or revenue, HR professionals should consider how the HR function can influence an organization's revenue. While an organization's sales team has traditionally been responsible for driving revenues, the quality of products and services and the servicing of customers contribute greatly to the ability to win and retain a customer's loyalty. Advanced sales effectiveness strategies link sales-force rewards directly to customer behaviors to develop sales or business development professionals. In addition, HR professionals can identify the talent capabilities and needs that are most effective in influencing customer behaviors in the areas of building customer relationships, product or service quality and innovation, or efficient production and delivery. In doing so, they can help create the processes, programs, and practices that optimize people in their efforts to net revenues.

As *bottom line* refers to the earnings, or revenues minus expenses, before interest, taxes, depreciation, and amortization fees are charged to the organization (EBITDA), HR professionals should consider a similar influence upon earnings. The efficient allocation of resources with minimal waste is essential to containing costs. Linking people behaviors to this effort is a collaborative opportunity for both HR and the business unit or functional leaders. In summary, HR professionals need to further grasp how each business function and its people contribute to revenue generation and the containment of the firm's operating expenses.

Also, the HR leader should understand the organization's profit pools, or rather its sustainable profit sources throughout the organization's value chain from the organization's chief financial officer (CFO) or finance team. The CFO can also provide an outlook for the organization's short-term (three-year) strategic plan from a financial perspective to provide the HR leader an appropriate context of the organization's direction.

- What are the organization's financial goals in terms of market valuation, profitability, revenue, cost, and market share?
- What business plans or activities are planned and what is the impact on the organization's financial structure?
- What is the greatest area of opportunity or risk that will impact the company's achievement of its financial goals?

Organizational Variables

Knowing How an Organization Exists and Competes

Organizations are born, thrive, and some eventually die. Conceptually, this life cycle is comprised of four phases: start-up, growth, maturity, and decline. The life cycle phase in which the organization exists greatly influences how an organization strategizes to compete in its market.

This concept was initially introduced by Mason Haire, whose 1959 work *Modern Organization Theory* applied a biological model to an organization's development. To elaborate, in the start-up phase, an entrepreneur goes to market with an idea and a fledgling organization grows with little structure and design but with great flexibility to move quickly in its development. In the growth phase, organizations gain momentum with market acceptance and begin to introduce structure and controls in order to organize people and operations. In the maturity phase, the organization is established with a competitive product or service within its market through a well-designed and organized entity. Finally, the decline phase is marked by a stagnant organization that fails to evolve within its competitive market by retaining outdated strategies, offerings, and operations that fail to deliver to a customer's changing needs.

HR professionals should be aware of the phase within which their organization exists and recognize how HR interacts with and provides resources to the organization in each phase. During a start-up phase, the emphasis is on attracting, acquiring, and retaining talent while setting an evolving structure. The growth phase is somewhat more complex as it may entail organic growth (expansion) or inorganic growth (mergers and acquisitions). Organic growth demands similar needs as in the start-up phase in finding talent whereas inorganic growth demands greater analysis upfront and potentially high-volume population absorption and retention on the back end of the project. The mature phase requires the HR leader to be highly cautious for risk that may upset the status quo and to be vigilant for opportunities to leverage the organization's human capital. Finally, the decline phase requires creative, innovative, and responsive HR skills as an "all hands on deck" posture prevails in an effort to bring the organization back to a competitive standing.

It is also important to know that each organization competes in its industry market to own profitable market share using one of three competitive strategies. These strategies are differentiation, cost leadership, and focus.

A differentiation strategy is competing in a market with a unique offering that differentiates the product or service from its competition, such as Apple in the personal technology market with unique products and services like the iPhone and the Genius Bar.

A cost-leadership strategy is competing in a market with the lowest cost structure in comparison to the competition, such as Wal-Mart has its stores positioned in the retail industry. A focus strategy is competing in a niche market as either a differentiator or cost leader, such as Cooper in the narrow mini-car segment of the auto industry with a very limited product offering.[26] An organization determines which of these strategies best suits its opportunity and available resources relative to the market and external influences. Some organizations attempt to employ more than one strategy with mixed results. A 2012 collaboration by Neiman Marcus, a luxury retailer, and Target, a middle market retailer competing on cost, is an innovative attempt to stretch both retailers' reach into the other's market niche and represents a blending of a cost leadership and focus strategy. However, history has shown that the most successful organizations become good at a core strategy and stick with it year after year, such as Merck in the pharmaceutical industry and HEB in the grocery industry.

Knowing the Organization's External Environment

The HR leader must look outside the organization to gain a better understanding of the external climate. The PEST (political, economic, social, and technological) Analysis assesses the current and possible external factors impacting the organization[27]

To complete a PEST Analysis, the HR professional, through a collaborative effort with others in the organization, identifies the major opportunities and threats in the relevant political, economic, social, and technological areas. Any findings within each area must be "one-handed," meaning that a finding can be only an opportunity or a threat, not both.

A PEST Analysis focuses on political, economic, societal, and technological aspects of the organization and market:

Political entails legislation that has been implemented or legal cases that have set precedent, such as new NLRB guidance (HR) or revised FDA regulations (organizational) that are relevant to the organization.

Economic entails macro- and microeconomic trends, such as rising inflation or decreasing unemployment rates in the areas in which the organization conducts business and its labor markets.

Societal includes significant trends in society in general, such as environmental sustainability or the broad use of social media that may impact the organization.

Technological includes significant developments that impact how a business operates or uses information, such as the advent of robotics and tablets.

Figure 4. PEST Analysis

Political	Economic
T- NLRB ruled against a company in the firing of an employee for social media comment	T- State regulations are capping emissions at revised levels
Social	**Technological**
O- Consumers are increasing their purchase of biodegradable products	O- Robotics have been developed for logistics

O = Opportunity T = Threat

Next, the HR professional completes a PEST Forecast to identify developing trends or changes in these same areas that may impact the organization and its industry in the future. HR leaders can complete the forecast by exploring any pending or upcoming decisions, actions, or initiatives that may drastically impact the organization's current business model. This may entail some hypothesizing and predicting based on current or past trends. In the end, the HR leader can engage other business leaders in this effort to gain a firm understanding of the external environment that may influence or control the organization's efforts.

Knowing the Organization's Internal Capabilities

As important as it is to understand the external influences that impact an organization, it is perhaps even more important to understand how an organization's own capabilities influence its existence. Through an analysis that identifies the current strengths, weaknesses, opportunities, and threats (SWOT) of the organization, the HR professional can gain this understanding. While strengths and weaknesses are internal to the organization, opportunities and threats are external to the organization. An organization can maximize its strengths and minimize its weaknesses to exploit the opportunities and contain the threats. Each element must be "one-handed." That is, an identified strength cannot also be identified as a weakness and an opportunity cannot also be a threat.[28]

Figure 5. SWOT Analysis

Strength	Weakness
All HR professionals are cross-functionally trained.	Staffing has no documented processes.
Opportunity	**Threat**
Employees believe that the services HR provides do not meet their needs	Unions have organized two competitors.

The organization SWOT Analysis provides the HR professional an additional perspective about the organization and its current state.

Organizational Direction

Assumptions Made About the Organization's Future

Strategic planning premises reflect assumptions about the organiza-tion's future. Referring to the external and internal analysis, HR pro-fessionals can identify and/or create premises that are differentiated by those that must be done from those that should be done in support of the organization's needs. Organizational leaders that develop premises use them as a basis for developing the strategic plan and can be broad (organization-wide) or narrow (function-specific).[29] Examples of strate-gic planning premises may be as follows:

- Emerging market demands that the organization consider adding new technology.
- Customer trends show that the organization must shift its prod-uct-based marketing approach to a service-based approach.

- Labor union legislation and decisions may increase union organizing activity in West Coast plants.

Understanding the Organization's Vision, Mission, Values, and Competencies

The company's vision should reflect a future state of existence in accordance with the direction the CEO wants to take the organization. The mission is very specific about what the organization is going to accomplish, and the strategy may be reflected through a set of strategic thrusts that embody the major actions that the organization must take to achieve its vision and mission. Here as well, HR professionals must consider the strategic HR imperative of optimizing people and their human capital as proposed in Chapter Three.

A vision describes the organization's future state of existence (three to five years out) in terms of what it will represent, how it will function, how it will profit, and how it will be observed by its constituents inside and outside the organization to include key stakeholders such as employees, customers, vendors, regulators, and competitors.[30] A vision is a realistic but optimistic view that must be meaningful for all stakeholders by defining a reality in which they see themselves as key to the organization's existence and success.

A mission articulates the who, what, where, how, and why the department will achieve its vision and the company's strategy.[31] A well-developed mission is tested when a team becomes entrenched with the tactical aspects of its function or mired in a debate of how to proceed with an issue or problem. If the mission is properly established, it serves to guide and realign their efforts.

With a developed vision and mission, an organization dictates the core values that are to govern how it conducts itself in its relationships with its stakeholders. Essentially, these are beliefs as to how an individual behaves morally and ethically that extends beyond even the organization. As previously discussed, a selfless leadership ethos should permeate the values of both the HR team and the organization as it serves the needs of its many constituents.

Finally, it is important to identify the core competencies required by the organization to execute the mission and achieve its vision. Given the industry, the markets, and the opportunities, these competencies may vary according to the needs of the organization, particularly with regard to its life cycle phase and competitive strategy.

Knowing an Organization's Strategy and Goals

The HR professional must identify the organization's three to five major achievements or broad initiatives to be realized in the next one to three years that will move the organization toward its vision. These thrusts will be a reflection of the environmental forecast, vision, mission, and planning premises or assertions.[32]

As it is challenging to try to accomplish everything that is desired or needed, organizational leaders must be deliberate and selective in determining the strategic thrusts through prioritization and resource allocation. The following are examples of strategic thrusts:

- Invest in new technology to innovate the product offering in entering the emerging market.
- Transform the marketing strategy and organization from a product- to a service-based effort in alignment with the business strategy.
- Develop and implement an employer–employee relationship campaign to improve people relationships across the organization and to reduce union-organizing threats.

From the strategic thrusts, the organization defines the key goals that are necessary to propel the strategic thrusts forward to realization in a shorter timeframe, typically within a few months. The goals are developed from the information gathered in the environmental analysis and from the mission and vision statements.[33] Essentially, the mission will be accomplished by collectively achieving these established goals.

At this point, the organization compiles the elements to create a strategic plan. The plan should include the following:

- Vision statement
- Mission statement
- Values statement
- Competencies statement[34]
- Strategic thrusts
- Major goals

Many organizations are capable of creating a strategic plan, but fewer organizations are able to successfully execute that plan. To do so requires plan operationalization. As a metaphor, a strategic plan provides a destination, a road map, and checkpoints to traverse along the journey; operationalization identifies the vehicle (operational) to use for the journey and the know-how to use the vehicle (tactical) to execute the plan.

In reviewing the major goals, the operational vehicles are the organizational functions and the knowledge, expertise, and skills of the function professionals. Combined, they provide the necessary resources and actions to achieve the goal. Once a strategic plan is created and communicated, the functional teams can create their operational plan.

First, the functional leader breaks each goal down into tactical objectives. Essentially, the objectives are sub-goals that collectively achieve the goal. The objectives may draw from one or multiple specialty areas.

Second, each objective is further separated into the tasks necessary to achieve it. This tactical execution relies upon the functional professional's knowledge, experience, and skills—their human capital.

At times, teams can become mired in the tactical aspects of their effort, typically due to a lack of expertise or resources. At this level, the functional leader must remove obstacles or provide resources to the team to ensure the tasks and objectives are completed. The devil is in the details in ensuring that a strategic plan is executed successfully, and leaders must recognize and overcome unplanned challenges. Just the same, functional leaders cannot get lost in the weeds as they must simultaneously remain focused on the longer-term organizational and department vision and strategy and delegate much of the execution to their team. The use of project management or planning tools is appropriate to help guide the team in their efforts to execute the strategic and operational plan.

Though the business concepts, influences, and strategy presented are briefly defined, through further study, HR leaders can develop a contextual understanding for optimizing human capital. Becoming an organizational pundit, or expert, is critical for the HR professional to effectively contribute to the business organization's strategy. But having the expertise is only impactful if it can be properly applied.

Principle Summary

HR's distance from the business discussion is due in part to a lack of relevant knowledge. Grasping business concepts, organizational variables, and organizational direction provides HR professionals a context for optimizing human capital. In doing so, HR is positioned to contribute more effectively to the organization's strategy and goals.

1. Does your HR team equally balance their HR expertise with their business expertise?
2. Where has HR's lack of business knowledge limited their contribution or effectiveness in serving the organization?

Principle #5:

Deliver HR on the Organization's Terms

Roseanna, a VPHR, had been on the job for a few weeks. She had met with every department leader, visited all of the organization's contact centers across the country, and had individually met with her HR team. Each time, she asked the simple questions, "What is HR doing for you?" "What is HR not doing for you?" and "What can HR do better?"

Roseanna learned from listening to executives, managers, employees, and her own staff about HR's strengths and opportunities. She learned about the organization's culture, its operations, its products, its competitors, its sales cycle, and its challenges. She had enough information to know in what direction she wanted to take her HR team with regard to supporting the organization.

Roseanna called her direct reports in for a staff meeting. In that meeting, she suggested to the HR team that they needed to reconsider their role and activities with regard to supporting the organization. Roseanna encouraged her team to consider the essential outcomes that an HR function provided to the organization. The answers were common to most HR teams, focusing on employee relations, staffing, etc. She pressed once more and asked, "Think about our clients and what they need from HR."

Just then, the vice president of operations knocked on the door and entered the room at Roseanna's previous invitation. His timing was serendipitous as Roseanna asked the same question of him. His reply was "I need HR to get me good talent, I need HR's help in developing that talent, and I need HR to help me retain my talent."

With a renewed focus on people and a new understanding about business concepts, organizational variables, and organizational direction, HR must consider designing a delivery platform model that takes these factors into account when providing services to the organization and its constituents. HR's current structure places emphasis on HR's functionality and provides support to the organization by a design that is suitable to HR's needs and frame of reference.

Without diminishing the expertise within the centers of excellence, HR can have a meaningful impact on the organization by reconsidering its structural design. That is to say that HR's current structure may not be the most effective design to support the organization. However, to consider a different design, HR must gain a better understanding of how it is currently perceived by the organization and its stakeholders. This requires HR professionals to understand how the organization's functions and stakeholders work toward achieving the strategy. For the purposes of this discussion, these organizational functions and stakeholders are identified as HR's constituents.

To gather the necessary insight from each constituent, the HR leader must gain a thorough understanding of constituents' goals, objectives, and necessary resources as they attempt to achieve the broader organization's strategy and mission. With this well-grounded understanding of each constituent, HR professionals can better know and understand how to design an effective structure, system, and the processes needed for HR to deliver on those needs and support the organizational direction.

Critical to this effort is first identifying and categorizing HR's constituency. Understanding the distinguishing characteristics of each group provides a context from which to operate HR. Each stakeholder is assigned to a group based on his or her role in the organization. This categorization is presented in the following figure:

Figure 1. HR Constituencies

Level	Constituency
Strategic	**Directorate/Owners** to include CEO, Board of Directors, and Shareholders
Operational	**Clients** to include C-Level/Functional Leaders and Management
Tactical	**Individuals** to include employees, candidates, organizational alumni, customers, vendor partners, and the general public/society

Directorate/Owners

It is important to note that the strategic directorate/ownership constituency has a critical responsibility and obligation to the organization's owners or shareholders. HR's direct relationship with the organization's investors is limited. Typically, the CEO and CFO take center stage in board reviews, investor relations, and market analysis. Nonetheless, emerging HR leaders must strategically and operationally grasp the strategic role the directorate/ownership play and understand the specific HR needs that will arise in support of this constituency.

As such, it is imperative for the HR leader to support the CEO and board of directors (BOD) in ensuring both a unity and continuity of executive leadership for the organization to achieve its goals into the future. To do so, the HR leader should be capable of providing input to the CEO and BOD in three specialized areas of interest: executive compensation, executive talent management (succession planning and development), and strategic human capital issues.

- *Executive compensation* requires a principle-based approach to balance owner–shareholder interests (increasing market value through asset optimization) and executive management interests (wealth accumulation through job security and success with minimal personal risk).[35]

- *Executive talent management* requires an understanding of both the short- and long-term organizational needs to hire, develop, and retain the requisite executive competencies and skills as well as the talent management program to deliver it.

- *Strategic human capital issues* such as macroeconomic and microeconomic trends and/or operational and tactical developments that may affect the execution of organizational strategy and direction is critical to the CEO and BOD as well. The development and presentation of a risk profile is also useful in keeping the leadership group aware of threats and opportunities.

Having this basic understanding of directorate/ownership needs can help shape the effort and services HR provides to this group. Keep in mind that each CEO and individual board member may see the role of the top HR leader differently than expressed in this viewpoint.

Operational

The operational group consumes most of HR's time and resources, but as it currently exists, it has been dominated by the administrative and transactional support HR provides. Functional department heads and their management teams within the operational group provide the planning, supervision, measurement, and utilization of the organization's resources toward achieving the organization's strategy and goals. Unfailingly, the most complex and invaluable resource that the operational group manages is people. Invariably, operational leaders view their people from two vantage points. One view is that of a *business resource* that provides a contribution to the organization through work duties and tasks to achieve a specific goal or objective. Another view is that of an *individual* who is paid, receives benefits, follows policies, uses paid time off, and whose personality, attitude, and choices at times create friction in the operation. The operational group works to balance such views and HR must assist in that effort to ensure that people-resources are optimized.

Tactical

The tactical constituent is comprised of individuals who are employees, vendor representatives, government entities, prospective candidates, customers, or any other individual who has a current, prior, or developing relationship with how the organization functions on a day-to-day basis. The most resource-intensive member of this group for HR, by virtue of its size and relationship to the organization, is the employee group. The new HR doctrine suggests shifting HR's dominating purpose away from servicing employees to optimizing their talent. However, HR must continue to provide excellent transactional services to employees to maintain a positive relationship in support of the organization's direction and strategy.

Vendors are essential as partners to fill voids where the organization does not possess the expertise or capability. Regulators are also important in ensuring that the organization functions within a legal, moral, and ethical framework. Candidates are not only those individuals identified within the organization's selection process, they can also be a broad and indefinable group. Any individual in any role not employed by the organization is a potential candidate, which is the broader population. This unique characteristic also transfers to the organization's customers. Customers are not only individuals or entities involved in an ongoing relationship with the organization through their purchase and use of its products and services, but also any individual or entity who currently has no relationship with the organization but who has the potential to purchase and use the organization's products and services, which may also include the organization's employees. This creates an expectation that HR, as well as the entire organization, interact with all individuals as potential customers, partners, and employees.

Fundamentally, a center of excellence is an expertise whereas an HR deliverable is the application of that expertise. If an expertise cannot be applied when and where it is needed, it is a misused advantage of nominal value to an organization.

Having identified and categorized each constituent along with valid assumptions about each group's identity, the HR leader can further differentiate engagement with each group. As the engagement with the directorate group, with the exception of the CEO, is unique and infrequent for most HR professionals, the focus on this group will not be elaborated upon further than what has been already discussed. As the engagement with the individual or tactical group hinges on the relational, this important engagement is to be further addressed in a later principle discussion. It is HR's engagement with the operational group that is most resource-driven and has the greatest influence on how people can contribute to organizational success. Thereby, it should influence how the HR delivery platform is designed. As the operational constituent is most essential to establishing a direction and for allocating the resources of the organization toward achieving its strategy and goals, their needs and concerns in performing their various functions should be integral in how HR designs itself to deliver upon those needs.

In assuming a resource-management approach with regard to an organization's people, it is important for the HR professional to know how a business unit and its people create value for the organization as was outlined in Principle #4. It is also important to gain an appreciation of the constituent's perception about HR's contribution to that effort. This can be most effectively accomplished through a 360° feedback process.

This can be done by simply conducting surveys, focus groups, or interviews to gather information about HR's past contribution, activity, and results. Listening to the voice of the customer establishes a baseline for understanding the constituency's needs. The HR leader can seek answers to these basic questions with the operational constituents:

- What does HR do well in supporting you, the function, the department's people, the customer, the vendor, etc.?
- What does HR not do well in supporting you, the department's people, the customer, the vendor, etc.?
- What can HR do to help you achieve your strategy, plan, goals, or objectives?

This process provides key information about how HR support is perceived and actualized. It allows for ideas and opinions that would not otherwise be known or shared about HR and its delivery model. On a personal level, in asking for this information, HR leaders must refrain from reacting to criticisms and assume a more inquisitive stance. Asking for additional explanation about certain statements is appropriate follow-up, so long as questions come from an investigative rather than defensive position.

These meetings should not be delegated. It is best for the HR leader to conduct these interviews personally and to keep the information received anonymous and confidential where deemed appropriate. Seeking feedback is advantageous in building credibility if used appropriately for the purpose of improving and implementing change. Keeping the information anonymous establishes trust with individuals who wish to remain unknown in sharing their comments.

As mentioned, the operational group most directly utilizes the organization's assets and allocates its resources to achieve identified goals. When asked how HR can support their efforts to sell, produce, deliver, and service the customer, business leaders will most likely focus on three basic requirements:

- Hire the best talent
- Develop the talent
- Retain the talent

These fundamental needs have a tremendous impact on an organization's ability to achieve its strategy by creating value for the customer. At first glance, HR professionals may not be surprised by this revelation—HR already provides for these needs through its talent acquisition/staffing function, its talent development function, and through its employee relations function. However, HR professionals must further reflect on these function's effectiveness and impact on the organization.

At this point, it is important to introduce the difference between the "push" and "pull" system concepts. In a push system, a producer or supplier pushes its products or services out to its consumer with valid assumptions about the consumer's needs. In a pull system, consumers pull what they need from the producer or supplier and the supplier accommodates.

Traditionally, the HR function has been designed as a push system when supporting the organization by dispensing its products, services, or advice to its constituents from a functional base. HR professionals may challenge this postulate as on a daily basis it is the organization's constituents that are pulling from HR with constant requests or needs in areas such as hiring, employee issues, or training. But, the reality is that HR develops and presents its tools and services as solutions to the organization most often through a one-size-fits-all structure and design dictated by HR's function-centric viewpoint. The operational and tactical constituents come to the HR specialty area that best serves their immediate need, then they request the resource or tool that is available as a solution to them, or pushed to them, in response to their needs. Any need outside what is available creates a gap and HR responds by finding an external resource or simply not fulfilling the need. HR's functions have been designed based on HR's capabilities and not necessarily based on the organization's broader need and interest. So what is an alternative to this broadly accepted, tried-and-true system?

Preferably, a more effective HR delivery platform within the new doctrine is based on a pull system. It is HR's constituency that must dictate what it needs from HR and pull it through and out of the department. More specifically, rather than structure HR based on functions, conventional assumptions, and beliefs, HR should be structured based on deliverables that the organization's constituents need to fulfill the organization's strategy.

Hence, the three core needs presented above must drive how HR structures and designs its function within a pull system concept. Additional design considerations include HR's cause and the strategic imperative of optimizing human capital. Also, it must be recognized that the three fundamental needs identified by the operational constituents are based in large part on their perceptions about HR's role. HR's constituents have been trained to see HR in a specific way. That is to say, the constituents view HR within the contextual boundary created by HR's functional design and ask for transactional assistance accordingly to what they know. This transactional need cannot be ignored, but the context in which it is given must be broader and constituents must be reconditioned to view HR differently.

Therefore, the transactional activity of hiring and developing talent are borne from a broader necessity of having the "right" talent doing the "right" things to execute the organization's strategy. Whereas these transactional activities are finite with a perceived beginning and ending, they are actually a component of a perpetual activity to ensure that the acquisition, development, and performance of an organization's people and the human capital they create is optimized to deliver on the organizational strategy and goals. As follows, HR must structure and design itself in support of a broader deliverable to optimize talent and human capital.

Retaining talent is a notional concept. Operational constituents understand that the retention of talent is critical to a continuous and efficient execution of their strategy and processes. Yet, their appreciation of the factors that contribute to retention is sometimes limited. One must only turn to Newton's First Law of Motion that states that an object at rest will remain at rest until acted upon by an external force and an object in motion will remain in motion at the same speed unless acted upon by an external force. Applicably, an individual will remain in a committed relationship with an organization until influenced by an external force or factor that disillusions him or her. Therefore, retention is a result or outcome of an effort to sustain an individual's relationship with the organization.

Although not explicitly requested as a basic need from the operational group, HR still must influence the environment and the tools individuals need to perform their work successfully. This entails how individuals both physically and intellectually work within an organization. The organization's workplace, equipment and materials, policies and practices, and systems and programs matter greatly to how effectively an individual is able to perform.

In the military, services members are deployed into a hostile environment with every possible advantage including equipment, policies, practices, programs, and systems that support their efforts and performance in a combat situation. HR should work to assist organizations to "deploy" their employees with every possible advantage to compete in their markets and industries. In this mindset shift, HR's transactional activities transform into a much greater influence on how successful employees can perform the work that they have been hired and developed to do.

Therefore, three HR deliverables emerge within the new HR doctrine to drive HR's contribution, structure, and design. They are optimization, sustainability, and deployment. Each of these HR deliverables is essential to the strategic success of the organization:

- *Deployment* ensures that individuals are able to perform their work with an advantage over the competition.
- *Optimization* entails the effective acquisition, development, and performance of people and the human capital they create.
- *Sustainability* includes the effort to sustain the relationship between the organization and the individual by protecting and retaining the organization's people and the human capital they create.

As each deliverable provides a unique contribution to the organization, they also share a synergistic relationship that when working effectively in synchronization, they produce a competitive advantage. As a deliverable, optimization yields the greatest impact to the organization's success as it is the application and execution of talent and human capital in support of the strategy. However, optimization is most impactful if people are deployed with a superior advantage against the competition and if a positive relationship between the people and the organization is sustained. The HR deliverables and their concinnity are illustrated in Figure 2.

As functional business units utilize the organization's assets and resources to sell, create, deliver, and service the organization's products and services with the customer, they view people as a primary resource to that end. The introduction of the HR deliverables creates an operational focus about people in the organization that does not detract from the tactical HR effort but rather leverages HR's transactional expertise for better alignment with its constituents' needs.

HR's transactional expertise grew out of the traditional HR-centric approach in which its centers of excellence influenced the way HR professionals structured their teams and departments. Through the HR deliverable concept, HR leaders and their staff are shifting to a customer-centric design and away from the traditional functional centers-of-excellence model. Fundamentally, a center of excellence is an expertise whereas an HR deliverable is the application of that expertise. If an expertise cannot be applied when and where it is needed, it is a misused advantage of nominal value to an organization. This transformative shift requires all HR professionals to refocus their resources, expertise, and efforts to a more strategically aligned effort with the organization and its customers.

Thus, the HR deliverables platform becomes the cornerstone of a revised structure. Within the new doctrine, HR specialty functions no longer work independently with occasional interaction when needs arise but regularly contribute their expertise, processes, and systems through a collaborative effort to ensure each HR deliverable is fully developed.

Figure 2. HR Deliverables

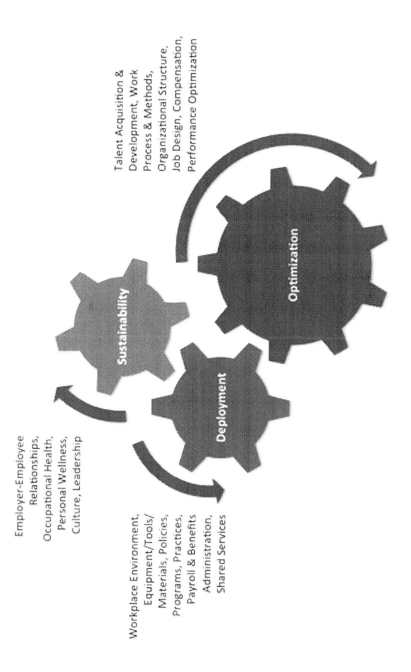

In execution for organizations with a larger HR department, functional centers of excellence continue to be important for expertise development, knowledge sharing, and compliance in order to ensure consistency of practice, policy, and philosophy. However, HR's success is measured by how successful its constituents are in achieving their goals. Rather than an HR leader presiding over HR's functional centers of excellence, an HR leader oversees the synergistic effort to deliver HR's expertise, services, and advice to support the organization's strategy. This further implies changes to the roles that HR professionals fill in the organization. As an example, a VP or director of optimization, deployment, and sustainability would take precedence over the traditional functional roles of VP or director of staffing, compensation, and benefits or employee relations. For smaller organizations, the HR deliverables remain more conceptual as guideposts with the HR leader focusing on ensuring that his or her work is organized to satisfy the organizational constituent's needs aligned with the three deliverables.

In addition to constructing an HR deliverable-based structure and approach, HR leaders must be resourceful in complying with laws, managing risks and data, and sharing information. Each of these areas can be categorized as functional HR "intelligence" in that they provide information and guidance to assist HR teams in delivering the HR deliverables. These intelligence functions may reside within a specific HR deliverable or as a stand alone entity within the department, but it should be considered a resource across the HR function. The HR intelligence areas are further described below and the deliverable that they are most associated with:

- *Human Resources Information System (HRIS).* HR teams have primarily relied on HRIS to create self-service platforms for employees and to provide minimal analytics. In the new doctrine, HRIS must be pointed toward broader opportunities in gathering data about employee skills, performance, and results. Additionally, the advent of social media and networks that exist both inside and outside an organization must be leveraged and

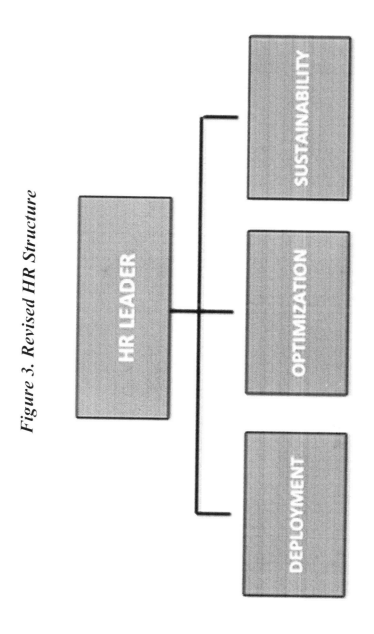

Figure 3. Revised HR Structure

HRIS must be capable of managing the technological aspects of these tools. *Deliverable: deployment*

- *HR Analytics.* The presence of a strong statistical competence within HR is long overdue. The technological age is providing organizations and individuals an unprecedented capability to collect and analyze data. Data can be used to analyze and identify opportunities for improvement, validate program design, and predict performance. HR must invest in a statistical competence to permit it to gain greater efficiency and effectiveness in its efforts. *Deliverable: optimization*

- *HR Marketing.* Marketing principles within the HR function is a need that should be considered more fully. Much as a marketing department promotes an organization's products or services, HR is responsible for promoting an organization's opportunity and culture to key stakeholders. Traditionally structured as internal communications outside of HR's influence, HR marketing entails developing a campaign to promote the organization's cause, direction, values, and its positive relationship with its people in order to drive engagement and optimization efforts. With HRIS's assistance, much of this effort must incorporate social media both inside and outside an organization. Despite the call by many labor and employment attorneys to curb its use in the workplace, social networking is a cultural juggernaut in the social narrative of human history. Just as it was used to ignite social revolutions in the Middle East in 2010, it can influence organizational efforts and contributions. HR cannot ignore such an opportunity and must embrace it. *Deliverable: sustainability*

- *HR Compliance.* Compliance is an expanding demand that requires a watchful eye for developing legislation, reporting requirements, and organizational guidance. Ensuring that a dedicated resource is committed to HR compliance is essential to maintaining a viable and productive optimization effort. *Deliverable: deployment*

- *HR Risk Management.* People risk is an ever-present reality that if not adequately managed can be a detriment to an organization's employment relationships and organizational capabilities. Litigation, unions, and physical injury are the result of a high-risk environment that requires a dedicated focus. A dedicated resource focused on risk can help to identify the organization's exposure and direct the efforts to reduce such risk where and when necessary. *Deliverable: sustainability*

The shift to an HR deliverables structure and approach is a tremendous undertaking and tendencies to default to the traditional approach based on functional centers of excellence shall persist, but the value that the HR deliverable structure and approach can add to an organization can be immense. Through this platform, HR inevitably becomes linked to the pulse and movement of the organization, proactively working with its constituents to produce optimal outcomes that enhance revenue generation, contain cost, and reduce risk. In addition, HR capabilities are further developed by functional and deliverable exposure that broadens the HR professional's experience.

Although the significant changes being recommended to HR's structure and delivery model may create more complexity in leading and managing HR resources, it does evolve HR to a much more resource- and execution-oriented function. However, how the HR deliverables are designed requires further elaboration. Nonetheless, the shift to this structural model and doctrine may awaken the sleeping giant within HR and breed a new HR professional with a greater influence and impact than previously observed.

Principle Summary

The traditional HR delivery platform is based on a function-centric perspective. Doctrinally, optimizing human capital necessitates a customer-centric platform. Analyzing HR's constituents to understand their needs leads to the development of HR's deliverables. The deliverables of deployment, optimization, and sustainment forms a new delivery platform basis.

1. In delivering HR, how effective is the current structure of your HR function?
2. How does your HR function ensure that it is meeting organizational needs through its current design?

Principle #6:

Design HR with the Organization's Customer in Mind

Upon arriving at his new assignment, Paul, an HR executive, was bombarded with requests from other executives, directors, managers, and employees who all had various unfulfilled needs. An interesting request came from Maria, a regional vice president (RVP) of operations.

Three years prior to Paul's arrival, Maria had invested in a leadership program from a well-known consulting firm. Each of the organization's business units had spent a small fortune purchasing a video set and individual manuals to train their directors and managers. The material was well received and Maria and the senior leadership team boasted success as nearly 100 percent of the leaders participated in the training.

Maria asked to have OD's leadership program restarted after a two-year hiatus. When Paul asked for more information about the program, Maria described how the program was comprised of several leadership training modules and that many of the trained leaders were still employed. She explained that the program was needed again because the newest supervisors lacked leadership skills and treated their employees poorly, as they claimed they had been treated, resulting in low productivity and poor product quality. The HR executive asked what qualified the new supervisors to be promoted. The response was that they were the team's most technically experienced employees.

Finally, Paul challenged Maria: "If the newest supervisors, who were led by the trained managers, are leading poorly, was the OD program actually a success? And how has the leadership program improved our product and service delivery to our customers? It appears the program did not address the underlying cause of the leadership problem as the leadership culture has not changed. Did this program truly improve the business? Did we satisfy customers and gain market share?"

The introduction of a new HR deliverable platform provides a tremendous opportunity to reorganize HR to more effectively meet the organization's vision and strategy. However, a new platform or structure is not just a reshuffling of functions under new grouping titles by HR deliverable. The design of the functions themselves must also be reconsidered.

This effort requires a systematic method to fully consider the important influences on designing HR's functionality. For this need, the HR/OD team can use a tool called the Human Capital Value Stream (HCVS). Essentially, the value stream outlines a flow that begins by focusing on the fundamental and most lucrative exchange of any business organization—the customer transaction or an organization's "moment of truth"—as this is the most critical and relevant interaction that directly impacts an organization's success. If the transaction meets a customer's expectations and can be successfully repeated at minimal expense, an organization can achieve its business and financial objectives and support its strategy to enhance shareholder value. Accepting this notion, the HR team can use reverse engineering to design HR's programs, systems, and policies.

The HCVS is comprised of four phases: *discovery, design, implementation,* and *optimization.*

Discovery Phase

As an organization's vision and strategy are aimed toward financial success, the new doctrine suggests a shift in HR and OD thinking to ensure that the organization's customer becomes the design driver as was suggested in the pull system discussion. This can be visualized as an inverted pyramid. In the inverted pyramid, the CEO or management is no longer being served at the top of the pyramid, but rather it is the customer at the top of the pyramid and those individuals closest to the customer who must be empowered and supported in their efforts to serve the customer through their work and outputs.[36] This is not a novel idea; the concept has been used in many organizations for

Figure 1. Human Capital Value Stream

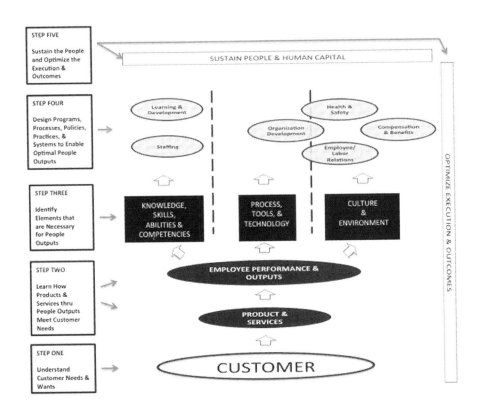

Figure 2. The Inverted Pyramid

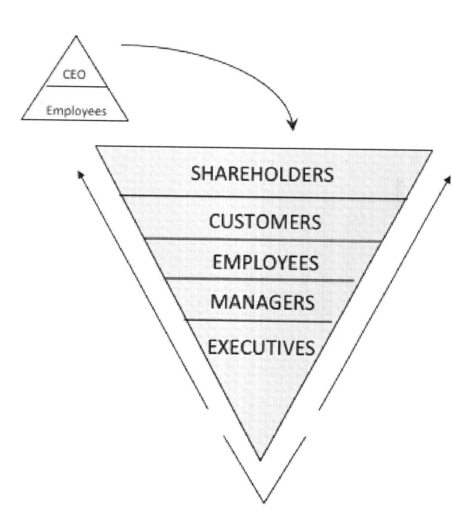

many years and has manifested into a servant-leadership approach. It is reasonably accepted that front-line roles have the potential to provide the greatest worth to the organization's value chain by virtue of their proximity to the customer. However, its application within HR has commonly stopped at the employee, not extending any higher in the pyramid.

HR/OD professionals must assume responsibility for optimizing people and the human capital they create as a resource in support of the organization's strategic direction and in further support of the customer relationship. As previously mentioned, human capital optimization is placing the "right" people in the "right" conditions with the best preparation to produce optimal outcomes to satisfy a customer's expectations. The underlying assumption of human capital optimization is that people have the potential to satisfy customer expectations through their performance if key elements and conditions exist by design and if obstacles are removed.

To further aid in the application of this thinking, there are four discovery needs necessary to form a basis for design.

The first discovery need begins with simply understanding the customer's needs and wants. This question captures the need:

What does the customer need or want from an organization's products and services—what is the "voice of the customer"? What attributes create value?

The organization's product or service has unique characteristics or qualities that make it a preferred choice. Whether it's the product's high quality or the immediate responsiveness of service providers, the customer values the organization's products or services. HR leaders can collaborate with the CEO or business unit leader, the CFO or finance leader, and the marketing team to understand these characteristics or qualities.

The second discovery need requires an internal analysis of how the organization produces the customer value. This requires an internal definition of the product and service attributes that meet customer needs and how an organization's people create them through key individual and team performance and outputs. This can be discovered by asking two questions:

a) What are the acceptable people outcomes that create value for external customers in terms of their needs and wants and how are they created?

Upon hearing and understanding the voice of the customer, there are specific people outcomes that satisfy the customer's needs. They may generally be defined as productivity, quality, service, and efficiency. Each organization has a minimum acceptable standard and a higher goal for performance. A standard satisfies a customer's expectations whereas a goal typically exceeds a customer's expectations. HR/OD's task is to collaborate with department and line leaders to define acceptable standards and optimal outcomes in the areas further described below:

- *Productivity* is the rate of an individual's output per unit of a specific input, such as time. On the surface, output is contingent upon the individual's ability to perform the perceived straightforward tasks necessary to reach an outcome. Realistically, an individual's ability is much more complex. An individual's ability can be viewed as a function of that individual's engagement, skill, and application. Furthermore, engagement is a product of satisfying the employee imperatives (relevance, meaning and purpose, and sustainment) that are introduced in a later discussion. Traditionally, productivity has been an internal operational excellence measure linked more closely to optimizing a capital asset such as a machine regardless of customer demand. Productivity should be balanced along with meeting delivery expectations of the customer with regard to timing, quantity, and product/service as an equally important measure.
- *Quality* is the measurement of an outcome compared to a standard. The measure of quality can vary from an objective to a subjective standard. Most importantly for organizations, the end consumer ultimately measures the quality of products or

services. Most often, human discernment is required to assess quality. This creates a tremendous responsibility for people charged with producing and assessing an outcome. Their commitment and focus must be unyielding to ensure that an organization upholds its reputation for excellent quality.

The underlying assumption of human capital optimization is that people have the potential to satisfy customer expectations through their performance if key elements and conditions exist by design and if obstacles are removed.

- *Service* is the advice or assistance provided to customers before, during, and after the sale of a product or service. It is the organization's "face" to its customers and must create feelings of confidence and satisfaction in consumers. Each service opportunity ultimately comes down to an interaction between an organizational representative and a customer. An infinite number of outcomes can arise from the interaction, either positive or negative. People who provide service must be counted on to embrace and believe in the organization and its products and services and work toward positive outcomes with empathy for the customer's perspective. This requires an individual ability that mirrors that of productivity in that it is a function of an individual's engagement, skills, and application.
- *Efficiency* is the ratio of an acceptable outcome compared to the resources expended to create the outcome. In producing a product or service, minimizing the cost and avoiding waste is essential to efficient production. Both service and manufacturing organizations must focus on waste reduction as a way to reduce the cost of creating a product. As a product or service can only be sold at a fair market price, any added cost strips away profit. People are relied upon to work efficiently in their efforts. Waste

can take many forms such as flawed product, idle machinery, injured people, mismanaged time, etc. People must be diligent in identifying and controlling such unnecessary costs.

b) What process responsibilities, duties, and tasks enable people to create these outcomes?

HR/OD professionals must become familiar with the key processes that lead to the production or delivery of the organization's key products and services. In doing so, they must assess the responsibility, duty, and task that each individual performs in the various processes in order to achieve a minimal standard or a higher goal expectation. The HR/OD professional must also determine the most effective method to measure the tasks and deliverables produced for use in continuous improvement initiatives.

The third discovery need entails the specific identification of the elements necessary to create the desired outcomes, including the knowledge, skills, abilities, competencies, processes, technologies, culture, and environment that enables people to create the most optimal results in terms of customer value. These elements are further categorized by HR deliverable in the design phase. However, this specific discovery effort will be further elaborated upon in the following sub-principle discussions.

The fourth discovery need is understanding the current HR state or situation. An HR leader can make arrangements to gather the thoughts, ideas, observations, and opinions from the tactical constituent group, which will primarily consist of employees but could also include candidates, vendors, regulators, and customers. In a straightforward manner, the HR leader can simply ask these two basic questions:

a) What has the organization or HR done or not done to support you in your role?

b) What could the organization or HR do differently to provide you greater support in your role?

The HR leader can also facilitate the HR staff in completing an HR SWOT analysis. Then, the information gathered from HR's constituents should be compared with the input provided by the HR team. How constituents perceive HR and how HR perceives itself may vary. This internal analysis provides awareness about HR's processes, policies, programs, and systems with regard to its alignment and impact to the organization and the external customer. Using information obtained from an organization SWOT analysis also provides the HR team an additional source of perspective about the organization it supports.

Design Phase

The HR team must create the methods that best serve the organization's efforts to deliver on the customers' needs. This involves a reverse engineering of the organizational and HR programs, processes, policies, practices, and systems. Rather than relying on functional paradigms to create the circumstances necessary to enable people to succeed, HR professionals must fundamentally understand the drivers that contribute to the customer need, value, and transaction such as people, processes, and systems.

As HR/OD professionals strive to design these elements and deliverables to deliver value to the customer, they must also consider how human capital optimization is actualized with regard to an individual or team by reviewing the model first presented as Figure 3 in Chapter Three. Each employee must be in a position to achieve optimal outcomes as they relate to a customer's expectations and the organization's vision and strategy. Ultimately, all of HR's activities and efforts must strive to have a line-of-sight connection through an organization's people to the critical customer relationship.

This also implies a shift in the priority of resource use. Whereas the services and attention expected in the employment of people remains constant, what limited resources are provided to HR/OD's efforts must focus upon the talent and roles that can most impact the customer relationship first and always.

Implementation Phase

After the design of a specific program, process, practice, policy, or system, it must be implemented. Implementation can be either simple or complex as there is an element of change and uncertainty to those it impacts. However, there are key elements to consider when implementing change.

First, it is important to explain why a new design is being implemented. This includes an explanation of why it is necessary to make the change in relative terms of importance to the organization and the audience. The impacted group must be given the opportunity to ask as many questions as needed to understand why the change is needed. The why can be generally explained by describing the current situation in terms of a challenge or an opportunity, what could be expected if a new program, process, practice, policy, or system is or is not implemented, and how it will impact all parties.

Second, it is necessary to set expectations through a thorough implementation plan. This should include explaining the purpose and the desired end state. This can be in terms of a measurable result or by what implementation success will look, feel, or sound like. In addition, it must be assumed that the more complex the change, the more necessary it is to phase the implementation with key checkpoints or decision points along a timeline to allow for progress updates, feedback, and adjustments. Communication becomes more critical the greater the complexity and the broader the impact of the new design. All impacted stakeholders must be party to the implementation to ensure that it is properly completed.

Third, it is helpful to issue coordinating instructions to all parties involved. This is needed to ensure that those who have key roles to play in the implementation understand when, what, and how to assist with the rollout. That is, if a specific individual or team must take an action before or after another action is to be taken, this ensures effective and efficient application of resources and talent to support the implementation.

Fourth, providing information about resource support is critical to ensuring that involved parties understand what, when, and how to access available resources. Under-resourcing will undermine implementation.

When change is resource intensive, it is even more important to ensure resources are properly arranged within the overall implementation plan at the right time and place.

Finally, an additional aid is the use of intelligence. That is, if there is pertinent information about potential aids, pitfalls, challenges, or short-cuts, this can be of great value to those implementing the design change. More information than needed is better than not enough information.

HR/OD professionals should work jointly with other business unit leaders to implement the resources, equipment, tools, environment, and conditions needed to successfully deploy employees into their roles, the organization, and the competitive market. As this is unique to each orga-nization, HR professionals are advised to not underestimate the impor-tance of the implementation phase.

Optimization Phase

Once implemented, there must be an ever-existing motive to opti-mize and improve upon the design. Measurement and analytics are necessary to ensure the function or process is yielding optimal outputs. Ideally, these will confirm that the desired people outcomes are aligned with the customer's needs and wants. This will be elaborated when explaining each deliverable in the following sub-principle discussions.

Through the HCVS, the elements of each HR deliverable are cre-ated. On a macro level, the value stream ensures that the customer drives functional HR design in a perpetual flow that adapts to the customer's expectations, competitive realities, and the resources available. In the sections that follow, each HR deliverable is created using the HCVS.

Principle Summary

The new HR deliverables precipitate a functionality design that is customer-centric. The Human Capital Value Stream (HCVS) tool guides HR professionals in a phased approach of discovery, design, implementation, and optimization. Through this approach, each HR deliverable's programs, systems, and policies are designed.

1. How has your HR function been designed?
2. How effective are your HR function's programs, systems, and policies in assisting the organization to achieve success?

6.1: Deploy Talent

Consider that in a time of war, military service members are deployed into a field of operations, or combat zone, to engage and defeat an enemy. Ideally in that deployment, service members are provided every advantage possible to succeed. This includes the equipment, tools, and resources that they use. It also includes a vast array of processes, programs, and systems designed to source service members with these items as well as fulfill their personal needs. And when possible, military planners attempt to create competitive advantages through the environment in which service members deploy, such as time, weather, and terrain as well as the use of principles of war that include the element of surprise and the massing of forces. Ultimately, the collective success of individual service members and their units increases the chance of the organization's overall success.

Comparable to military service members, business organizations hire and deploy people into a competitive market. In that market, they are tasked to win over consumers for the products and services the business creates, sells, and delivers by luring them away from the competition. However, in many business organizations, leaders practice an approach that renders most employees, except those in direct sales or service roles, to work within the confines of an established structure and role under a set of procedures, policies, culture, and environment that are detached from a belief that each employee can impact the organization's relationship with its external customers. When realistically, all employees contribute to an organization's strategy and plan and impact the external customer's perceptions and expectations, and if not, then they should. As such, and in direct comparison with a military service member's deployment, each employee must be deployed into this competitive market with every possible advantage to succeed. Through a more specific application of the Human Capital Value Stream (HCVS), the variables to consider within the organization and HR's control when deploying employees into this competitive market field can be better defined and integrated into the deployment deliverable.

Discovery Phase

What resources, systems, equipment, tools, environment, and conditions best enable the successful completion of these responsibilities, duties, and tasks?

Despite this being a question more suited for front-line leaders and managers, it is important for the HR/OD professional to understand all areas that impact an individual's ability to perform. The HR professional must inventory all elements both inside and outside of HR's traditional function scope that directly influences the employee's ability to perform optimally. This inventory may include, but is not limited to, the following:

- Workplace environment
- Workplace policies, programs, and processes
- Work equipment, tools, and materials
- Workplace systems

Traditional HR functional areas that fall within this inventory are payroll and benefits administration, human resources information systems (HRIS), and employment handbook or policies. Nontraditional areas include workplace design, workflow planning, equipment design, and material planning.

Once identified, the HR professional must work to understand the link between each element and its influence on optimal performance. If resources, systems, equipment, tools, environment, and conditions are not adequate or not available, then people cannot produce an optimal or sustainable product or service of the highest level. HR/OD professionals may not be the party to remedy the shortcomings, but they should be actively engaged in recognizing, identifying, and communicating them to the appropriate parties and providing assistance whenever possible.

In completing this discovery phase, HR professionals should interview employees performing the tasks, supervisors facilitating the process, and managers planning the operation. In this interviewing process, questions must be asked about ideal resources, equipment, materials, tools, environment, and conditions as they pertain to creating optimal results. The answers must be used to determine a consensus of what employees, supervisors, and managers identify as enabling them to create optimal outcomes (low or bright lighting, tablet or smartphone, in-person or electronic communication, etc.). These are quite simplistic "either–or" questions as there are more in-depth elements to consider, but the main idea is having those closest to the customer dictate what enables them to perform optimally.

Design Phase

Design the programs, processes, policies, practices, and systems that create the environment and conditions for individuals to perform and create optimal outcomes.

Much as in the military, an effective deployment of people entails a thorough design and plan of resources, environment, and conditions linked to the employee's front-line effort. In this effort, past paradigms about HR functional design must be suspended. Although HR's centers of excellence provide valued expertise, the fundamental differences are in the design's purpose and the measurement.

Realistically, all employees contribute to an organization's strategy and plan and impact the external customer's perceptions and expectations, and if not, they should.

Here is an example of the subtlety of this difference. In conventional HR design, a process is typically designed to fulfill an organizational need such as hiring or offering benefits. Additionally, a law is designed to protect employees from employers doing them wrong. Thus, an HR program is designed to fulfill the need and comply with the law. HR measures its processes success by auditing for legal compliance and counting number of hires and speed of hire or benefit plan participation and cost savings.

Alternatively, in this new doctrine approach, HR learns that customers buy products that require exact technical specifications. Given this need, HR designs staffing or benefit programs with functional business unit leaders to acquire, develop, and engage employees who provide technical expertise in creating value for the customer through their work. HR also designs the programs with adherence to moral, ethical, and legal standards to ensure the employee remains in a state of mind to perform successfully and to ensure the program complies with the law. HR measures the programs' effectiveness less by transactional activity and more by the employees' performance outcomes, customers' behaviors, the organization's financial achievements, and risk containment.

The same design work is completed in either scenario. Even though process and program design based on business needs seems to deprioritize legal demands, the mindset shift represents a renewed focus on creating value for the customer and in turn optimizing the organization's people to serve that customer. HR expertise is to be applied in ensuring this effort satisfies legal requirements or moral and ethical standards but not as its exclusive purpose.

In this effort, optimal performance can be best achieved with resources, in an environment, or under conditions that are most conducive to success. Having effective and well-maintained equipment, processes, and resources within a work environment designed to promote work efficiency and effectiveness as well as under conditions that sustain human needs can significantly differentiate an organization from its competition.

The following demonstrates how some of these facets impact an individual's success:

- Optimal performance can be influenced by the policies written and enforced by organizations and HR departments. Drafting policies that explain what behaviors are not acceptable may be limiting in contrast to writing policies that explain the behaviors desired. Rather than establish a rule-based, "catch me if you can" policy approach, HR/OD professionals should strive to influence a guideline-based, "follow me and do as I do" approach that promotes a positive rather than a punitive approach. This by no means eliminates the need for HR to address undesirable behavior or outcomes, but it can be assumed an organization focused on what is desired rather than what is not desired will influence people in a positive direction.
- An organization's environment may actually have the most influential effect on people producing optimal outcomes. Elements such as resource accessibility, workflow design, built-in security and safety, ergonomics, information sharing, communications, color, furniture, and natural lighting have a tremendous influence on an individual's ability to work effectively. HR professionals and organizational leaders must also avoid a one-size-fits-all approach. Some organizations that have abandoned offices and walls to convert to an open floor design find some people are less effective and productive as the distractions of other conversations and activity limit their preferred work style. A balance must be sought in any effort.
- Environmental design may also involve time, location, magnitude of effort, and control. Depending on the nature of an organization's operation, it may be possible to employ a remote workforce, allowing people to work from a location and at a time of their choosing. This enables efficient and effective work while maintaining a connection to the organization and protecting its interests. Regardless of where or when the work is done, HR professionals must pay close attention to the impact an organization's environment has on its people's ability to produce optimal results.

Implementation Phase

Refer to the implementation discussion presented in Principle #6.

Optimization Phase

Measure and improve the designed programs, processes, policies, practices, and systems and their outputs.

As previously defined, optimization is making the best or most effective use of a resource. To do so, the resource and its outputs must be continuously monitored for effectiveness in delivering on expectations. In this effort, HR/OD professionals must work closely with marketing professionals to understand the customer's response or activity with regard to the organization's products and services. Any discovered deficiency in their attributes defined through the people outcomes described in Step Two of the HCVS Model solicits a need to work with functional leaders to identify and eliminate the underlying cause.

As noted, HR is to measure the programs' effectiveness less by transactional activity and more by the outcomes. This is not to say that transactional activity is not important to understand the efficiency of effort, but it is not representative of the impact upon the organization's success in achieving its strategy. Employees' performance outcomes, customers' behaviors, the organization's financial achievements, and risk containment all come to the forefront in this renewed deployment effort.

Deploying people with a superior advantage is essential to organizational success. As employees assume their roles within organizations, it must be assumed that competitors are assigning their employees to the same roles and all individuals compete through their contribution to the organization through their performance. If an employee can be provided the superior resources, equipment, tools, environment, and conditions, then a large portion of the competitive battle for the customer is won.

6.2: Optimize Results

As organizations and teams work to achieve their strategic and operational goals, they procure and utilize tangible, physical assets such as equipment, machinery, and facilities. Through a vetting process, they study and determine which assets best serve the needs of the organization and then purchase them. Teams inevitably face a time when an asset fails to produce or provide the output that it was designed and procured to do. Because of the investment made in acquiring the asset and the opportunity potential to generate a value in support of the organization's strategy, teams set about trying to repair the asset. Most times, they do so through a methodological process. First, they troubleshoot to identify and isolate the underlying root cause. Once the root cause is discovered, the team brainstorms a solution to eliminate, reduce, and/or contain the problem to bring the asset back on line. The team further measures the asset's utilization with regard to its efficiency, output, and quality and attempt to find the correct settings and conditions for optimal performance.

This is the manner in which shareholders gain value from the assets they own in an organization. The value is derived by how those assets are optimized by management as mentioned in the advocacy discussion. In this doctrine, an organization's people and the human capital they create also can be considered an asset. Therefore, it too can be optimized. Where a physical asset is procured, modified or prepared as necessary, positioned, operated, maintained, repaired, and optimized, similarly people can be acquired, developed, deployed, sustained, and can be optimized to create value.

This concept falls squarely in the functional HR areas of organizational development (OD), talent development, and talent acquisition. There is little to add to the wealth of concepts, approaches, and tools that already exist in these areas. Furthermore, it has been realized over time that a synergistic relationship exists between these functions. It is this relationship that is being further emphasized within the optimization deliverable. Through the discovery phase of the Human Capital Value Stream (HCVS), the functional variables and their interrelationship can be better articulated to understand their influence on optimizing talent and human capital.

Discovery Phase

What knowledge, skills, abilities (KSAs), competencies, work processes, organizational structures, and job designs best enable the successful completion of the necessary responsibilities, duties, and tasks?

The HR/OD professional must, in collaboration with the functional leader, begin to form assumptions about the KSAs and competencies that people apply to work methods and processes that create these optimal outcomes. To do so, an exercise that allows key stakeholders to have input in narrowing the KSA and competency list is necessary. That narrowing should result in a final list of KSAs and competencies that substantially contribute to creating optimal outcomes. These KSAs and competencies form the basis of HR's talent acquisition process and talent development program design. Invariably, the KSAs and competencies must be routinely measured against the expected outputs to ensure their relevance and importance is validated.

Optimal performance is the product of not only personal capabilities but also of process, structure, and job design. Traditionally, the design of these elements has been dictated by business functions with minimal HR input. However, HR must take an active role in ascertaining how influential and impactful these elements are in optimizing performance. Studying work process flows, organizational/team interaction, and job tasks and duties can yield a greater understanding and appreciation for how outputs are produced and how they can be optimized.

Design Phase

Design the programs, processes, policies, practices, and systems that successfully acquire and develop the talent and create the processes, structure, and jobs necessary for individuals to perform and create optimal outcomes.

Talent acquisition involves finding individuals who are capable of mastering the required KSAs and competencies with an acceptable fit to the organizational culture and environment in order to create optimal outcomes. Methods and approaches to identify candidates inside and outside of the organization are plentiful and each organization must identify the method that best delivers upon its needs. However, the method chosen must be designed with a time period that balances candidate "shelf-life" and business demand, must balance the cost with more costly steps taken later in the process, and must be completed by individuals who have an intimate understanding and appreciation of the job role, required KSAs and competencies, work processes, and customer needs.

Regardless of how effective or efficient a talent acquisition process can be, organizations are limited in learning how effective an individual will be in a job role prior to the individual assuming the role. A capability gap essentially exists on the date of hire. However, this gap is often overlooked by HR teams. Traditionally, development efforts are in response to identified KSA or competency shortcomings as requested by managers well into an employee's tenure. HR/OD professionals must design a development program that immediately trains new employees in the required KSAs and competencies to enable faster and better opportunities to close the capability gap. This elevates the relevance and importance of the KSAs and competencies in how directly they influence the creation of products and services that the customer values. Therefore, talent development and acquisition are inextricably linked together in having employees master the required KSAs and competencies to create optimal outcomes that directly impact organizational success.

Work methods and processes are key in that through their design they enable the creation of optimal outcomes. Each method or process must be designed to effectively apply employee capabilities to available resources to efficiently create optimal outcomes. In many organizations, HR/OD professionals have shied away from this critical element in their efforts to enhance performance effectiveness. However, the synchronization of capabilities, resources, and processes is essential to optimizing performance. HR/OD professionals must work with their business unit partners to design the process workflow and tasks that best utilize the employee KSAs and competencies to create customer value.

Further within the work method and process design is individual job position design. Each job must be designed with each task, duty, or responsibility area necessary to achieve the desired outcome. Whereas OD professionals have placed emphasis on job design to ensure employee engagement through task variety and significance, they must equally balance job design with customers' perspective with regard to their desired products and services and the necessary performance and business processes to produce them.

Finally, organizational structures have often been formed and maintained without much consideration to changes in processes, technologies, or people capabilities. HR/OD professionals must determine what type of organizational and team structure best enables employees to deliver on customers' needs. As an organization's structure can take many forms, it is important to understand the structure's impact on an individual or team's ability to produce. Some leaders are committed to a traditional, hierarchical structure while others are committed to a flat structure and still others are committed to a matrix organization. HR/OD professionals should consider the process, activity, tasks, and outcomes of an organizational unit to determine what structure is most conducive to optimizing the team's ability to deliver its product or service. One structural approach may not work for all units within an organization.

Implementation Phase

Refer to the implementation discussion presented in Principle #6.

Optimization Phase

Typically, the attention given to employee performance has either been through performance management systems, punitive disciplinary approaches, or alternative methods based on key performance indicators (KPIs) with a muted link to customer value. Conventional performance management methods have become an ineffective chore rather than a performance enhancer. Past performance management efforts focused on completing an annual evaluation process typically imposed upon the managerial ranks to substantiate compensation planning efforts that were focused more on employee prosperity rather than the fulfillment of customer or organizational needs.

Also, the influence of work processes and methods in performance management have been minimalized. Furthermore, differences in roles, work, and outcomes have often been ignored in favor of an annual, one-size-fits-most performance management approach. Punitive approaches do not necessarily result in an improved and sustainable level of performance but have rather focused the organization on separating an employee with the least risk to the organization. Finally, KPIs often measure operational process efficiencies rather than results that truly measure customer value. HR/OD professionals and the organization must adapt in how they approach performance.

By one definition, performance is the action or process of carrying out or accomplishing an action, task, or function and by another the capabilities of a machine, vehicle, or product when observed under particular conditions. In this doctrine, employee performance is defined as the effectiveness in applying an employee's capabilities to carry out or accomplish an action, task, or function under particular conditions to achieve an established standard or expectation with an organization's customers.

Optimizing performance requires measuring performance relative to the influence on a customer's behavior. That behavior is the customer's acceptance, purchase, repeat purchase, and increased volume purchase of the organization's products and services. This requires a revisionist view on HR's workforce analytics. HR pundits have already promoted the case for HR metrics and workforce analytics as a necessity for HR's strategic role. However, typical approaches to workforce analytics focus on broad descriptive metrics that describe a workforce attribute, such as turnover or headcount, or general inferential measures that infer a relationship between that attribute and another metric, such as revenue per headcount. Both types of measure reflect information that is diagnostic for financial analysis or for describing the workforce status in an organization. However, a renewed focus should include measurement of the effectiveness of an organization's programs and its people in creating the desired outcomes that meet customer expectations or organizational goals.

Customer analytics provide a measurable profile of customers' preferences and behaviors, both positive and negative. Much as considered in designing HR, understanding what the customer likes or dislikes serves as an indicator of how effective individual capabilities, work processes, structure, roles, and outcomes are in achieving desired results. Using available customer data from the marketing team and from other business functions such as operations or supply chain that regularly measure people effectiveness within its measurement of operational excellence, HR/OD professionals should identify the factors that sparked a positive customer reaction to reinforce and exploit their influence by integrating them into the appropriate design elements. Just as well, HR/OD professionals should identify and investigate the causes that provoked a negative customer reaction.

Optimizing performance requires measuring performance relative to the influence on a customer's behavior. That behavior is the customer's acceptance, purchase, repeat purchase, and increased volume purchase of the organization's products and services.

Also, by using data measurement and analysis, HR/OD profession-als can have greater efficiency in the use of limited resources. By focus-ing on those issues identified as most impactful to the customer and organization's goals, HR/OD professionals can apply the "80/20 rule" by spending roughly 80 percent of the resources and effort on the 20 percent that matters. This is an important point to stress as OD organi-zations have become heavily vested in senior leadership development. Inherent to this reallocation of resources is that senior leadership and managers' development will be secondary unless directly related to cus-tomer-facing matters. The assumption is that developing the leadership abilities for senior leaders is an inefficient use of resources and a reflec-tion of an inadequate leadership-selection process. However, invest-ing in senior and middle-management leaders to expand functional or industrial knowledge or to resolve a functional leadership attribute, or the lack thereof, that is negatively impacting the value chain or a cus-tomer relationship is a better use of limited resources. Otherwise, lead-ers should develop their personal leadership attributes at their own cost as an expectation of their employment.

With this increased focus, HR/OD professionals can ensure that the people fulfilling these roles or activities are provided the following support:

- Performance evaluation
- Feedback and input
- Reinforcement or improvement

Performance evaluation is subject to the nature of the individual's work and proximity to the customer. Work nature can be either project- or activity-based. As the doctrinal definition of performance implies that there is a beginning and an end to performance, this is actualized as a performance cycle. Comparatively, roles closest to the customer have shorter performance cycles in comparison to roles farther from the cus-tomer that have longer performance cycles. Evaluation, feedback, input, reinforcement, and improvement must be more frequent with closer proximity and more involved with project-based work. Evaluation must be linked to a customer's behavior in an objective manner using a rating scale as to contribution impact, KSA/competency application, and values alignment.

Reinforcement requires HR/OD professionals to consider a compensation model that bases its merit increases on organizational results with a "go or no-go" expectation about an employee's effort, specifically their work ethic, values, and alignment. Variable pay should then be used to reward contributions that have a meaningful and measurable impact on creating value for the organization by satisfying financial objectives to generate revenue, contain cost, and increase earnings through influencing the customer transaction. Ideally, variable pay should be designed with a mix of monetary and nonmonetary rewards. The nonmonetary rewards should be designed to satisfy employee imperatives. Many organizations are already implementing a "pay for performance" model that places greater emphasis on how variable pay is allocated. The new doctrine further suggests evolving to a process that evaluates the impact rather than the effort in a "pay for results" model as the next step in variable compensation planning.

Where improvement is needed for an individual's performance, a process improvement approach should be used to identify and resolve underlying causes that detract from optimal execution and performance results. As was discussed, when a tangible asset like a machine or piece of equipment does not perform to standard, troubleshooting is conducted to identify the potential underlying causes. Once identified, an effort is made to remedy the shortcoming and get the asset back on line. Similarly, HR and business professionals must investigate the reasons why an individual's performance is less than acceptable and improve how people function or how people are supported as part of the solution. Where managing performance closest to the customer has often devolved to a disciplinary approach for underperforming front-line employees, optimizing performance focuses on identifying opportunities to realign employee performance with customer expectations and organizational goals.

Operational functions have far outpaced other disciplines, to include HR, in the area of process improvement. Adopting quality improvement programs first authored in the United States and implemented in Japan after World War II, production and supply chain business units have further adopted each evolutionary step in process improvement from total quality management to Six Sigma to Kaizen to 5S to lean systems. While there are many methodologies that are used for process improvement, all are founded upon the assumption that a process can be more effective or efficient than its current state. HR must adopt this assumption in optimizing people as an asset. But how?

Quite simply, once an improvement opportunity is identified from accurate and consistent data measurement, most process-improvement methods follow specific steps. First, define the problem and scope. Second, measure the relevant outcomes and process. Third, analyze the relevant data to form a hypothesis about the problem and to identify the underlying root causes of the problem. Fourth, brainstorm and implement solutions to fix the problem. Finally, measure the results. A process-improvement approach will be a significant tool for HR in optimizing performance.

A practical method for HR may follow closely with the Six Sigma approach first developed by Motorola and made popular by GE. Although more appropriate for highly measurable processes, Six Sigma's methodology can be adapted for performance optimization needs. However, any process improvement method should also engage key stakeholders by leveraging social networks developed within the organization to assemble as many thoughts and ideas as possible throughout the process. This overall process improvement effort influences an investigative approach with solution generation rather than a conventional approach designed to assign blame and punish under-performers.

The following is a simplified tactical process improvement example using the concepts presented in the book *The Six Sigma Way*.[37]

1. **Define the problem, issue, or opportunity.**

   This must be done in an objective manner through a project charter and problem statement that includes the voice of the customer, the responsible team, the critical outcomes, the measures, and the timeframe. A problem statement may be similar to this example:

   AMEX customers are dissatisfied with the level of service provided. An initial review reveals that service levels for the AMEX client performed by the account team are an average 4.68 points below standard (97.7) over a period of three months (2/1/10- 4/28/10). This cost the company a 5 percent penalty fee.

   Where relevant, working with operational teams to map the process or procedure using a flowchart can help identify the order and elements of each step to determine potential issues.

2. **Measure the outcomes.**

   Determine the relevant data to measure. This should include both inputs and outputs of the process in order to better understand the issue. Then collect the data. This is an example of data related to the problem described in the example above:

Table I: Sample Data Sample Data from AMEX Team

Date	Team	Score
2/3/10	Smith, Jones, Garcia	87.56
2/7/10	Jones, Garcia, Ostrowski	94.32
3/17/10	Smith, Garcia, Okapo	98.56
4/2/10	Jones, Okapo, Ostrowski	96.64
4/19/10	Ostrowski, Smith, Okapo	92.41

3. **Analyze the data.**
   Identify the gaps that exist between actual results and expected results. Identify inputs such as team members, date of events, time of day, KSA mastery, etc. At this step, HR professionals should consider the cause-and-effect links between these variables. Determine the potential opportunities that exist to improve people's inputs and the obstacles that may hinder their efforts.
   A basic tool to determine potential opportunities to improve or identify underlying causes and effects is a fishbone diagram. Using this tool, HR professionals can investigate if the underlying cause lies within one of the following prescribed categories:

- People:
  ○ Knowledge, skills, abilities (KSA), or competencies
  ○ Culture and environment
  ○ Human behavior (i.e., attendance, failing to meet a standard of conduct, or motivation)
- Method: structure, processes, procedures, and work practices
- Materials: supplies and resources
- Machine: equipment and tools

As demonstrated in the fishbone diagram above for the identified performance issue, an investigation of people, materials, method, and machine may entail the following considerations:

- People: If an individual is not able to do the job, then HR professionals must explore if it is an ability or an engagement issue. If it is an ability issue, then the acquisition, development, and deployment processes and tools should be investigated. If it is an engagement issue, than people needs or imperatives must be explored and areas such as compensation, payroll, benefits, and other people-related programs are to be reviewed if relevant. If the culture or environment is not conducive to performing the job, then HR professionals must isolate cultural or environmental

160

Figure 1. Fishbone Diagram

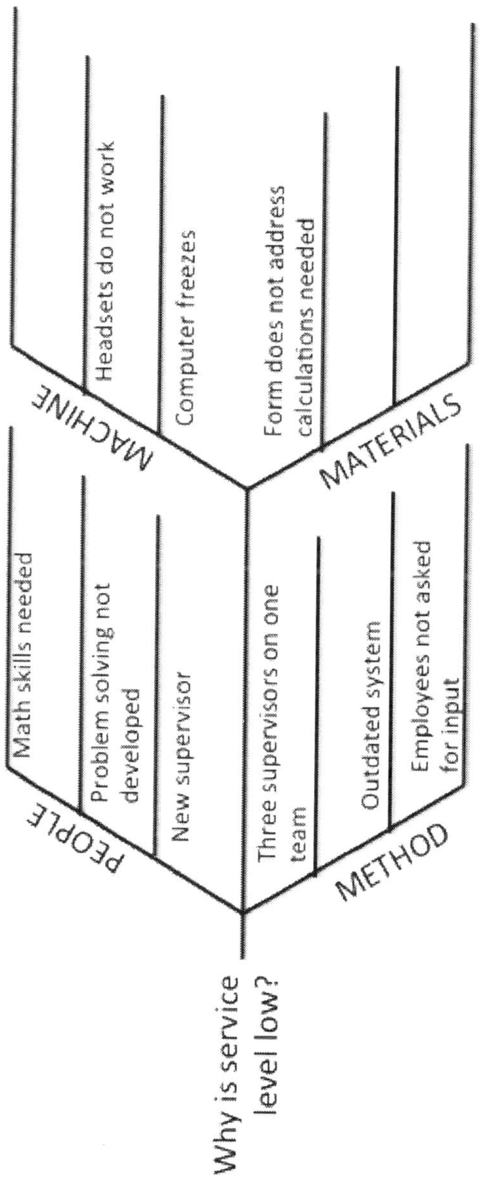

MACHINE

Headsets do not work

Computer freezes

Form does not address calculations needed

MATERIALS

PEOPLE

Math skills needed

Problem solving not developed

New supervisor

Three supervisors on one team

Outdated system

Employees not asked for input

METHOD

Why is service level low?

influences, such as leadership, structures, values, facilities, programs, etc., to understand what is undermining efforts.

- Method: If structure, processes, or systems are not permitting work to be completed, then HR professionals must work with team leaders to determine the reasons that may be limiting work effectiveness.
- Materials: If the appropriate materials, supplies, or resources are not available or usable, then HR professionals must work with resource providers to ensure that they are made available and are usable.
- Machine: If specific equipment or tools are inadequate due to lack of repair or unfit for the work's purpose, then HR professionals must point this out to find a remedy with the appropriate parties.

In its simplest form, identifying underlying root causes involves asking why at least five times. This "five why investigation" scrutinizes an existing condition by peeling away each layer of potential causes until settling on a base root cause:

- Overall service levels are low. Why?
- Because service levels are low in credit processing. Why?
- Because a new credit process task is being done poorly. Why?
- Because team members lack adequate math skills. Why?
- Because math was not a required skill in hiring. Why?

It is necessary to identify the root cause of the problem in order to focus improvement efforts and avoid recurrence of the problem.

4. **Design or improve the process.**
   Once the underlying causes are explored, HR professionals must use their wisdom and judgment in determining which area or issue has the greatest impact on the problem and make it a priority to resolve. Once determined, the HR professional works with others to brainstorm solutions that will eliminate or reduce

the underlying root cause. This may be a change to inputs, a change to a step, the removal of an obstacle, or a creation of a new process.

For this example, solutions may include the following:

- Eliminate credit task
- Shift credit task to another role
- Add math skills to acquisition and development process

When a solution is identified as the most optimal, implement the solution with a plan of action. The plan of action should define an objective, the tasks and resources needed, and the end state desired.

5. **Validate the improved process.**
   Once a solution has been implemented, it is necessary to measure the outcomes to determine if the desired improvement has actually occurred by referring back to the external customer, the "voice of the customer." If the desired results have not been achieved, then the HR professional must repeat the analysis. Even after a desired end state is achieved, HR professionals must continuously measure the outcomes to sustain them.

The quantification of work can represent a formidable challenge to implementing a performance optimization approach. Just as challenging is the quantification of results with regard to customer behavior when many competing factors influence results. Where performance management relied on a subjective assessment despite efforts to objectify it, it is more difficult to quantify an individual's work outputs specifically when outputs are the result of an integrated process or as part of a team. However, when a faulty product, shoddy service experience, or lost customer sale is reported, HR/OD must be a resource to examine, analyze, and resolve the people aspects of the issue. HR's opportunity is to create a reliable method or process to measure people's performance and use it first and foremost to improve the results by optimizing and improving the performance.

Optimizing human capital is not only in the design, implementation, and execution of programs, processes, policies, and systems, it is also in the continuous monitoring, improving, and maintaining of optimal performance. All HR efforts must aim at ensuring people are in a position to produce the most optimal outcomes to ensure that the organization succeeds in winning and retaining its customers' business and ultimately achieving its strategy. Thereby, the new doctrine suggests ending the management of performance and beginning the optimization of human capital.

6.3: Sustain Human Capital

A sustainable resource is defined as a resource that replenishes at a pace equal to its use. Organizations use great discipline to sustain their resources in order to utilize them for an extended period of time. In most cases, these resources are equipment, buildings, machinery, or other physical objects that can be used to generate value. In essence, people are a sustainable resource in that as they create outputs, they are also able to learn and apply new concepts and ideas to generate further outputs. Much like other resources, organizations can also sustain people to generate value over an extended period of time. This may seem exploitative, but the actions to sustain people are and should ever be to ensure the individual is performing successfully and that requires the individual to have his or her needs considered and fulfilled.

Sustaining people as a resource entails both the protection and recovery of people from physical harm or illness as well as preserving the human capital that they create. Whereas the former is mostly about the risk involved with people working within an organization and managing that risk, the latter is about keeping people engaged with the organization to leverage their knowledge, skills, and experiences.

Discovery Phase

What culture and relationships best enable the successful completion of the necessary responsibilities, duties, and tasks to create optimal outcomes?

HR/OD professionals must investigate the cultural foundation that supports optimal people outcomes. Employees can disclose what cultural elements enable them to perform at their best. With this insight, every facet of a culture must be analyzed including values, communication, and relationships to understand how they support optimization.

165

But it is also important to form a basis of understanding about the individual employee.

In addition to being *capable* of creating human capital, people must feel *compelled* to do so. However, being engaged precedes being compelled. Unfortunately, some HR professionals have been described as *not* being about people and this perception is somewhat borne from HR missing opportunities to adequately engage and compel people to act in alignment with the organization's needs and direction. Although some organizations have grasped the strategic advantage of engaging their people, other organizations and HR professionals must learn to understand the factors that influence engagement to create and sustain it. Three potential factors include what people need and want from an organization, how people evolve within an organization, and how an organization relates to its people. In short, people are sustainable resources so organizational efforts that address their personal needs, employment, and relationship with the organization are vital to sustaining a competitive advantage through its people.

The Employee Imperatives

Physicians and psychologists study people in an attempt to explain how the brain and psyche affect individual motivation and needs. From an experiential outlook, a workplace perspective is proposed that adds to their body of work. For people to be engaged with an organization and the work they do, they must be focused without distraction to accomplish optimal outcomes. Any distraction reduces this engagement and, in turn, reduces the potential for creativity and productivity. Individuals who have their workplace needs fulfilled have greater potential to be engaged. Most people in a society share similar workplace needs. These needs are defined herein as "employee imperatives," in that without their fulfillment the likelihood of engagement and organizational success diminishes. It is essential that HR professionals understand the imperatives as their existence contributes to the optimization of the organization's human capital.

The employee imperatives are *relevance, meaning and purpose,* and *sustainment.* Whether it is a new individual on his first day at the job or a tenured veteran in her final weeks of employment, each individual has basic imperatives that are essential to engagement with an organization in an effort to create optimal outcomes. If individuals or teams feel relevant, understand the purpose and meaning in their work, and are adequately sustained, they can accomplish difficult tasks even in extreme circumstances by their sheer loyalty and commitment.

These three imperatives create an emotional, intellectual, and physical basis for wellbeing. Wellbeing in turn creates healthy self-esteem and confidence that can potentially result in engagement, creativity, productivity, and longevity (retention). The importance and value of employee imperatives will vary by individual, based on personal circumstances. Nonetheless, each imperative exists to some extent in an individual's conscious or subconscious mind. This premise holds that people who believe they are relevant, who have meaning and purpose in their work, and who are able to sustain a preferred lifestyle have a higher potential to succeed.

Relevance

Irrespective of position, status, personality, or demographic, most people want to be regarded as relevant in their lives and this is predicated on their relationship with others. That is to say that most people want to be respected by others with a regard for their being or existence. The struggle for relevance can be witnessed across generations within our society. Teenagers seek relevance as they labor to transition and be accepted as young adults and the elderly seek relevance as they strive to not be cast aside and forgotten. This need is ever important to a person's ego as, without it, many people may react adversely, particularly to the source of their discontent. Sadly, in its worst manifestation in the workplace, people can grow angry and sometimes aggressive in their reactions with less than desirable results such as workplace violence or third-party representation, while still others withdraw from exposure to others' indifference and their contributions reflect this disengagement. It takes only one example of callous disregard or indifference by an individual to another individual in the workplace to undermine that individual or team's effort and progress. Ultimately, people seek a basic respect from others regardless of their station in life and for others to uphold their dignity in whatever situation may arise. Basic relevance is important to individuals even at their most vulnerable moments.

Relevance within an organization can also be derived from individuals being valued for their thoughts, ideas, suggestions, efforts, and contributions. This value arises from the individual being asked to contribute to an effort and being recognized for that contribution. Not only is a basic personal relevance satisfied, a greater relevance to the organization is gratified. This serves to reinforce an individual's efforts and desire to be creative and productive in an organization.

In support of this opinion, Marsh & McLennan was asked by one of its clients to conduct a pay study to understand the impact of pay to its turnover of customer service representatives. After gathering data on turnover, promotions, job changes, and external pay, a statistical model was created to predict why workers quit. The results showed that pay raises only shaved a half point off the turnover rate and that workers did not feel underpaid, but rather dissatisfied. They found that frequent changes in tasks and duties, even without pay increases or formal promotions, made its high-performing employees stay with the company.[38] It could be concluded that workers who were provided job-related changes based on their abilities and past contributions stayed with the organization longer as they were made to feel relevant to the organization.

People are sustainable resources so organizational efforts that address their personal needs, employment, and relationship with the organization are vital to sustaining a competitive advantage through its people.

In many organizations, relevance is an absent notion. Much of the focus is placed on motivation to influence results. Efforts to motivate individuals with contests, prizes, or rewards are often undermined because basic relevance has been ignored. Despite it being a rather easy and straightforward offering to bestow, organizations often overlook it. Relevance need not come from extravagance but rather from a simple conveyance of respect and gratitude. Being made to feel relevant inspires people to contribute rather than motivates them to act. Inspiration can be defined as being stimulated to feel or do something from within, whereas motivation requires an extrinsic reason for an individual to act or behave in a certain way. Consequently, people who are made to feel relevant are inspired to have a deeper and longer commitment to the organization compared to individuals motivated by short-lived initiatives in the form of prize or punishment.

Furthermore, relevancy can be reinforced when an organization's leadership communicates openly and regularly with its people. When individuals believe that they are informed about their organization and their role in it, they have a high trust and regard for the organization. This spurs engagement and drives individual success. Therefore, relevance is a contributing factor to an organization's success.

<u>Meaning and Purpose</u>

In his role as president and CEO for a consumer goods company, successful international business executive Juan Fernando Roche shared his wisdom through a commonly told story about how people approach work. He told the story of two masons who were toiling away at laying and setting bricks in a wall that stood in a clearing of land inside a small village. A stranger had wandered into the village and stood and observed the two individuals working for a short amount of time. The stranger approached the first mason, who was working in a disgruntled and frustrated manner, unhurriedly setting the bricks stacked before him. The stranger asked him, "What is it that you are doing?" The man replied in a dejected and sour tone, "I've been hired by our village leaders to come here and build the walls for a new church. I am out here all day in the hot sun, laying brick after brick, and working my fingers to the bone for a pittance!" The stranger nodded his acknowledgement and walked further down the wall to the second mason. This individual was working with much greater efficiency and whistling while he mortared and set each brick in what seemed like a seamless and effortless routine. After a few moments, the stranger asked him, "What is it that you are doing?" The second individual cheerfully replied, "I have been asked by our village leaders to help build a house of worship that will one day be a great cathedral for the people of our village!"

Though an unembellished tale, Mr. Roche's rendition illustrates how meaning and purpose have powerful consequences in how individuals approach their work. Meaning and purpose is formed predominantly by how individuals interpret circumstances compared with their values framework. In the story, the first individual's apparent indifference to the work at hand may stem from the fact that the work did not align with his values framework, thereby offering no meaning or purpose to him. Perhaps work in designing the church, or landscaping the church, or being the minister, or building a military fort may have more meaning to the individual than the work he found himself doing. In contrast, the same work provided exact meaning and purpose to the second individual as it was aligned with his values framework and skills.

Often, people do not articulate a need for meaning and purpose in their work, but where it does exist, a higher level of engagement and effort is evident. One must only look to the New York City police and fire departments whose officers' and firefighters' belief in the meaning and purpose of their roles to serve and protect their citizens led to their brave ascent into the World Trade Center towers to rescue those in harm's way on September 11, 2001. The meaning and purpose of their work was obvious, but how can this be replicated in jobs and work that may be, on the surface, as basic as laying bricks and mortar to build a wall?

The reality is that most individuals want to believe that their daily efforts are meaningful and purposeful, whether in or out of the workplace.

Meaning validates effort. Purpose satisfies ambition. The importance of each will vary by individual. Furthermore, it has been broadly discussed that younger generations entering the workforce want meaning in their work and want to contribute to a higher purpose.

The challenging task of sustaining engagement can be more easily accomplished if individuals find meaning and purpose in their work. And although each person must determine if his or her work has meaning and purpose, an organization should provide meaning by articulating that work's contribution to a higher and enduring purpose. To do so requires the organization to communicate a vision and strategy that can be linked to a well-defined purpose or cause. If that link can be effectively made, then finding meaning in work is made ever more possible for that individual. Albeit, this may be harder for some organizations to accomplish (hedge fund companies who buy sub-prime mortgages to create collateralized debt obligations to sell risk to unsuspecting investors) versus others (cancer research hospitals), it requires that each organization reexamine its strategy and goals and identify how what it creates serves a higher purpose.

For example, a ballpoint pen company manufactures and sells pens that appear to have little purpose in life's scheme other than being writing instruments in a technological age. But, consider how the pen is the instrument used to sign treaties that end wars, or to sign bills into law, or to sign a mortgage loan for a family to buy a new home, then it becomes an instrument used to transform life at many levels. In reality, the pen is an instrument of peace, justice, and prosperity. In this way, an organization can identify its contribution to a higher purpose.

After creating a vision with purpose, organizations that routinely communicate that vision to their people increase the opportunity for individuals to find meaning in their work and, in turn, spark engagement that creates opportunity for optimal outcomes. To further reinforce, the organization's leaders may also coach individuals one-on-one to identify a link between their personal job tasks, the company's broader purpose, and their values framework. Through their decisions, behaviors, and actions, organizational and HR leaders can influence an individual's belief in the genuineness of the job's meaning and organizational purpose. Also, leaders who, by example, selflessly subordinate personal agendas to serve an organization's purpose enhance their people's support of that purpose—a contributing factor for organizational success.

Sustainment

Compared to previous generations, many people today are placing a heavier emphasis on work–life balance. This has increased the importance of basic needs that an organization has the potential to provide through the third imperative of sustainment. As an organization employs people for their talents and contributions, in turn, it provides resources for individuals to sustain their work–life balance. Specifically, organizations can assist individuals through financial wellbeing, wellness, safety, security, and time.

Organizations offer employees compensation and benefits in exchange for work. However, providing an income and benefits to employees may no longer be enough to sustain and retain the best of them. Financial wellbeing is a broad concept that takes into account the ability to create and sustain a desired lifestyle. Consequently, if an organization can provide the tools and resources to help individuals accumulate wealth and financial wellbeing rather than just earn an income, their engagement and contribution will be strengthened. Realistically, accumulating wealth and financial wellbeing depends on making good judgments and personal choices to create an affordable lifestyle while avoiding insurmountable debt. Not only can an organization contribute to this effort by paying fair compensation, it can offer resources to help individuals wisely organize their finances to sustain a realistic lifestyle with aspirations for financial wellbeing. Other compensatory offerings such as variable pay and 401(k) plans with company match go further to help individuals accumulate wealth. Otherwise, the lack of financial wellbeing can have harrowing consequences that detract from individuals' focus and engagement and in turn their contributions to the organization.

Despite health trends that indicate otherwise, most people desire to be in good health. Many people do so by making good choices about lifestyle, diet, and exercise, or their general wellness. To fulfill this need, many organizations have implemented wellness initiatives that drive and reward healthy behaviors. However, many HR professionals find it difficult to explain the return on investment for such programs to business leaders.

Typically, wellness programs are measured by their impact on absenteeism, turnover rates, and improved productivity. However, wellness programs must be further measured by the impact they have on achieving financial goals such as cost containment and earnings growth. Exercise and diet choices are very personal and it may well be a challenge for organizations to influence these choices in a way that's acceptable to employees. However, poor health is a drain on an organization's competiveness in the marketplace and must be seen not as an arbitrary circumstance but as something that can be influenced or controlled. If not, poor health creates a distraction that hinders employees' success through their missed contribution to an organization; this creates a business disruption.

Physical safety and security in the workplace is paramount to individuals' ability to engage and produce optimal results as well as provide for themselves and their dependents. A safe and secure workplace with conditions and practices that protect the physical and mental wellbeing of people is essential. This includes a culture free from exploitation, harassment, discrimination, and violence. Workplace injury, illness, or abuse severely impedes people from effectively doing their tasks and renders them incapable of sustaining themselves and their dependents.

Too often, organizations allow a high-risk culture to develop with unspoken expectations that people get the job done with little regard for physical or mental wellbeing. In the short term, these efforts produce results, but they are unsustainable as they fail to regard the individual's relevance, purpose, or sustainment needs. Should physical or emotional harm be incurred, the HR professional must provide direction and oversight on how to recover effectively while also assisting in sustaining the operation. This entails developing strong relationships with an organization's people, insurance carriers, and healthcare providers. An organization that protects its people from physical harm and mental anguish creates confidence and security among its team members that yields greater engagement and outcomes. HR professionals must work to influence their organization's culture by creating sound safety, health, and wellness practices and accountabilities.

Finally, people value time, particularly when less is available for use or when competing demands exist. Whether it is the time to accomplish today's obligations or to fulfill one's lifelong dreams and plans, its value is personal and based on the worth an individual places on the activities or opportunities to use the time that's available. Organizations recognize the value of time as demonstrated by paid and unpaid time-off policies, but they typically fail to embrace its worth in optimizing relationships with people.

Time policies are designed to control an individual's time away from work for planning purposes rather than for keeping individuals engaged to achieve optimal outcomes. However, some organizations have abandoned such policies and have reverted to an open policy in which individuals manage their time at and away from work with more emphasis on individual outcomes or business results.

Realistically, an organization's characteristics will dictate its time policies. For example, a manufacturing organization must rely on planning for production schedules whereas a marketing organization must rely on creativity for client campaigns. The former requires a measure of control on its people's time at and away from work whereas the latter requires an outcome by a deadline indifferent to the use of time.

All individuals experience events or activities that are either planned or unplanned that compete for their time. When organizations deny time off as a punitive measure, individuals impacted are at risk of becoming disengaged. Organizations that express trust and empower their people to self-manage their time while simultaneously assuming responsibility for achieving expected outcomes may gain levels of engagement unprecedented since before the 1970s. HR professionals must creatively design a time program that links the organization's goals and the individual's needs while minimizing business costs and disruption and optimizing employee engagement.

The Employee Life Cycle

Much like other resources, employees have a unique resource life cycle that typifies their existence within an organization. Being a sustainable resource, people's development and engagement must be monitored and reinforced when necessary to ensure the optimization of their performance and continuous learning. Throughout their life cycle, individuals develop based on the influence of their experiences and by circumstances. Individuals' development is reflected in their level of effort and contribution to the organization. Organizational leaders and HR professionals can help create experiences and circumstances that positively influence an individual's development, but there are also dozens of other influences from other employees through interactions, situations, and observations that occur during employment.

Conceptually, the employee life cycle is based on three underlying assumptions. First, that individuals become engaged immediately with an organization upon first contact. Their engagement evolves over time, varying in its level of intensity based on the before-mentioned influences and circumstances. Second, after joining an organization, people develop their skills, knowledge, and experiences—their human capital—over the same time frame. Third, if individuals' engagement and human capital can develop in a positive direction over time, then the opportunity for optimizing outcomes and retaining talent in the organization increases. Figure 1 shows a graphical representation of this relationship.

However, the reality is that an individual's engagement is not always developing in a positive manner. Events and interactions may influence a negative development. The struggle between these alternating influences weaves through an individual's employment period. The life cycle is comprised of three periods; a short pre-employment period, an open-ended employment period that is further classified into four distinct

Figure 1. Engagement: Human Capital–Outcome Relationship

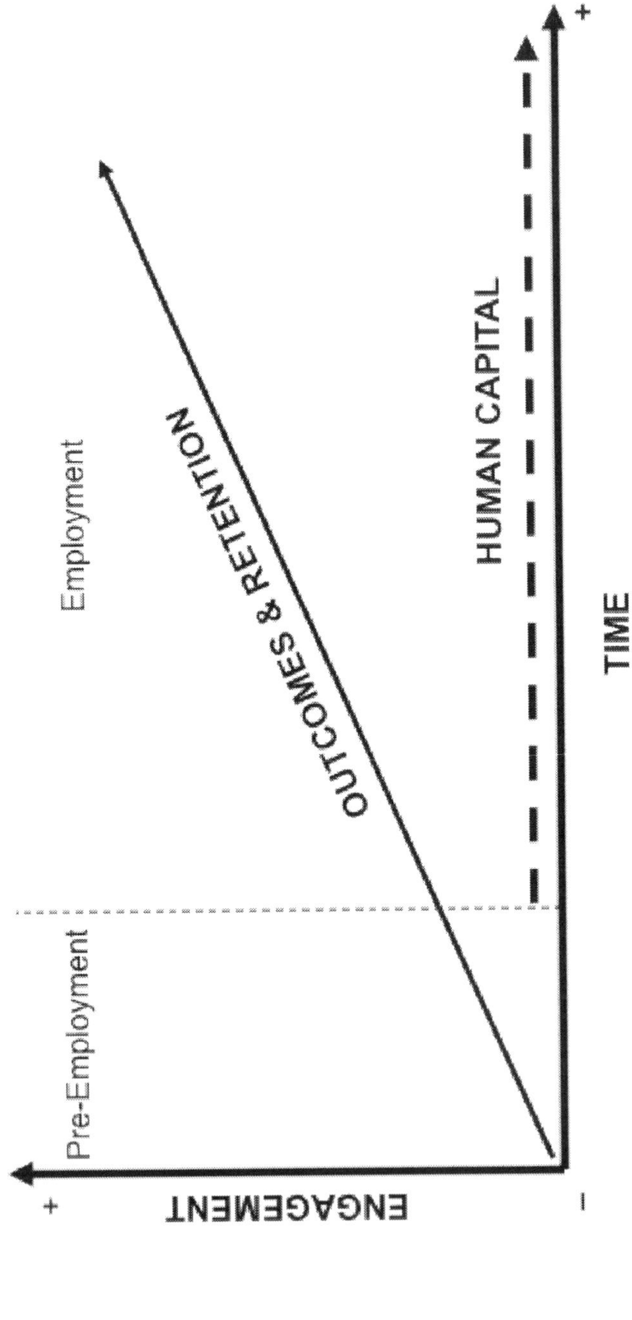

phases, and a post-employment period. Each employee is unique and each has a different experience within an organization. Nonetheless, the employment experience described in the life cycle is common to many employees.

Pre-Employment Period

The employee life cycle begins prior to joining an organization. In this pre-employment period, the first contact event brings both parties together as the organization is searching for a team member and the individual is searching for employment. The contact can be active or passive and can occur through any variety of communication channels: face-to-face, phone, e-mail, text, Internet, or advertising. First impressions are critical for both parties. This contact begins the recruitment phase in which the individual and the organization evaluate each other to determine if they can meet each other's requirements. The flow of information in both directions is crucial as long-term relationships are being developed with these initial impressions. The desired output of this phase is the selection by the organization of an individual to join it and the individual choosing the organization that best matches him or her in terms of ambition, abilities, and needs.

In the recruitment phase, organizational leaders must create a campaign to attract individuals to the organization, differentiate from other organizations to be the "choice" using marketing principles, and identify, vet, and select "best" qualified candidates.

Individuals in this phase have two essential goals: to make an informed decision about joining the organization and to secure a position that satisfies their needs.

Employment Period

The recruitment phase ends with a hiring decision and the employment period begins with on-boarding. On-boarding's purpose is to introduce individuals more intimately to the organization. Development, knowledge sharing, and relationship building begin immediately with the goal of having an individual contribute effectively as soon as possible. This is done through communication, orientation, and basic training.

Communication includes the individual's leader reaching out to welcome the individual and set early expectations about the first day and first few weeks. Leaders should also answer any questions an individual may have without prejudice. The leader's goal is to establish the foundation for their relationship and the employee's relationship with the organization.

Company orientation programs most often include both the administrative employment requirements and an introduction to the organization's history, purpose, culture, structure, programs, and values. Organizations often fail to appreciate the impression made on new employees who are vigilantly observing every aspect on this first day. Also, organizations should grasp that employees must have their needs and concerns answered before any other message is presented. Questions concerning personal matters such as work schedules, break areas, lunch, parking, or paydays must be answered within the first several moments of employment. If not, it creates a distraction that shifts employees' focus away from the program.

Although much has been written about designing orientation programs, in the context of the new doctrine, there are four critical attributes to consider in designing an orientation program:

1. Preparation: Failing to prepare gives an impression of a poorly organized company and a disregard for the importance of new employees.
    a. Have required documentation or systems available.
    b. Have team members and key staff briefed and ready.
    c. Set agenda with efficient use of time and maximized learning (avoid overloading and use interactive activities).
2. Delivery: Capturing the hearts of employees on the first day builds meaning, purpose, and engagement if properly communicated.
    a. Design with organizational branding.
    b. Link to organization's vision, mission, strategy, and values.

Figure 2. The Employee Life Cycle

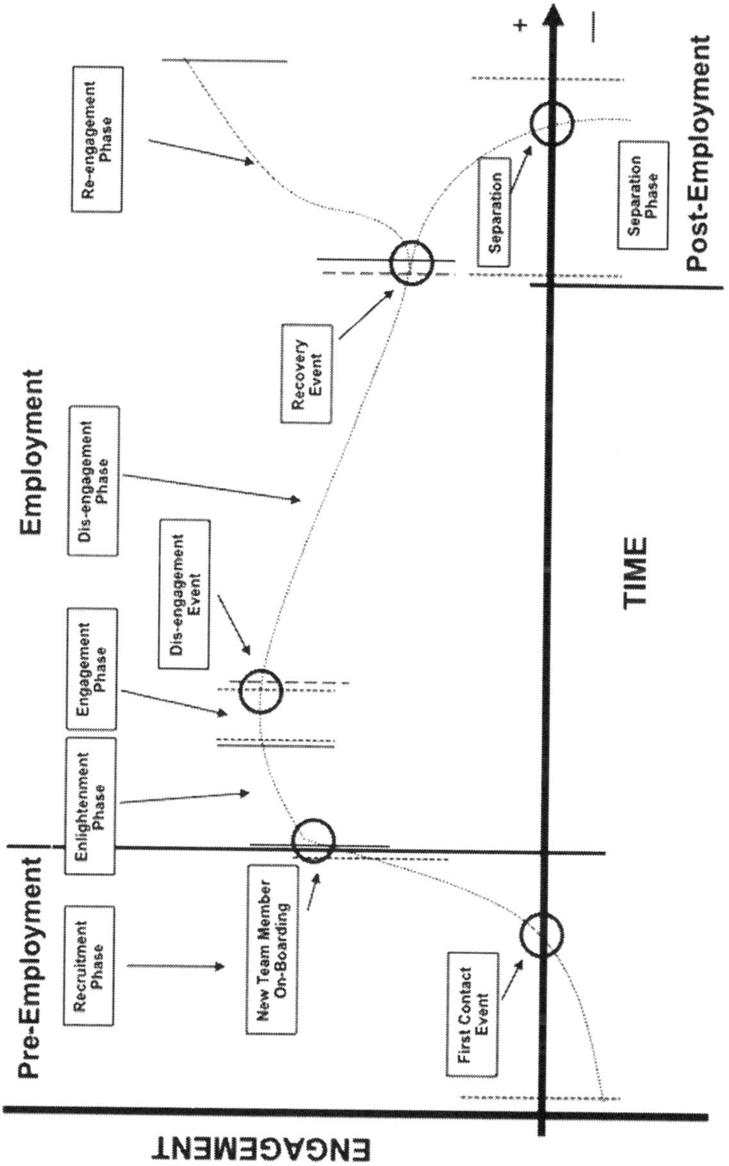

3. Impression: Not unlike an effort made with customers to brand an organization's products or services, organizational representatives must act, speak, and interact with the newest employees to reinforce the organization's culture in making first impressions.
   a. Lasting impressions are made in the first two minutes of employment.
   b. Continue to market and sell opportunity to individual throughout employment.
4. Relationships: Despite good intentions, leaders too often make building relationships with team members a low priority; this can be negatively interpreted by new employees as their being unimportant to the leader. The leader must do the following:
   a. Be the first to meet the new hire.
   b. Ensure introductions are made to other team members.
   c. Become the primary point of contact.
   d. Assign a reliable sponsor or escort.

Most often, basic training formally introduces the individual to the specific job role, responsibilities, duties, and tasks. It presents the required skills and competencies and begins to build the individual's capabilities. This is a critical baseline requirement for optimizing the individual's performance. The individual's leader needs to be involved in the training even if a training department exists to begin setting expectations that are to contribute to performance optimization.

After the brief period of on-boarding, employees enter into the enlightenment phase. In this phase, the individual is continuously learning through practical, hands-on experiences but is still not quite functioning at the most optimal level. Also within this phase, the individual is being culturally indoctrinated by fellow team members, informal leaders, and by events and situations. The key output of this phase is to have the individual fully engaged with the organization and contributing optimally.

Key leader actions in the enlightenment phase are the following:

- Conduct a goal-setting meeting with the individual:
  - ○ Prepare and discuss the team's mission, goals, and objectives.
  - ○ Discuss performance and conduct expectations.
  - ○ Present the team's communications, reports, and other tools.
- Communicate with individual to monitor progress and needs.
- Model correct behaviors to counter any negative influences, reinforce values and principles, and build meaning and purpose.
- Recognize and reward performance achievements and encourage correct behaviors.
- Assist the individual to reach full engagement and optimal contribution sooner in the life cycle.

During this phase, individuals are still finding their way and assessing the organization and their status. Most individuals work hard to impress their leaders, as they can be self-conscious of their job security in these uncertain first several weeks. However, the individual is also forming opinions about the organization as to centers of influence, informal structures, and cultural inconsistencies. Peer pressure to conform is also revealed and the individual has to find a path to fit into the organization on both formal and informal levels.

The next phase is the engagement phase and is typified by a fully functioning individual who is at or near peak performance capability and effectively contributing to the team's success. The key output of this phase is sustaining and retaining an individual's engagement for the long term.

Key leader actions in the engagement phase include the following:

- Engage the individual with meaningful and purposeful work.
- Ask for the individual to participate or provide input through additional assignments or project participation.

- Match individual strengths and interests to work opportunities where possible.
- Prepare individual for next-level roles or broader or different current-level assignments.

During this phase, individuals are the most engaged. They are fulfilled with their job as they are effectively contributing to the team and they have confidence in the organization, their leader, and themselves.

Sometime in the employment period, the inevitable threat of discord arises in what is termed a disengagement event. This event creates a risk to the organization. People become disengaged in their role because of the following potential issues:

- Boredom in limited job scope or task variety
- Inability to use skills or competencies
- Loss of confidence in organization or leader, typically due to values and principles being compromised
- Employee does not see alignment between current state and career aspirations
- Peer pressure to conform to alternative culture and values
- Needs and imperatives not being appropriately met or addressed
- Employee is made to feel irrelevant due to lack of respect or recognition

This event leads to the beginning of a disengagement phase that may occur at any time during the life cycle. The individual is engaged minimally and outcomes suffer with lower productivity, poorer quality, poorer service, and inadequate efficiency. The individual appears bored, distant, indifferent, or frustrated. The key output in this phase is to reengage the individual by managing the risk as previously outlined.

When leaders recognize the disengagement phase, they should begin an informal investigation of the underlying causes of the individual's disengagement and create a plan of action to reduce or eliminate the cause and/or obstacles to engagement.

Leaders must know that during this phase individuals are contemplating or actively searching for another role within or outside the organization. They have the potential of becoming a greater risk in two ways: they can become a negative influence on the team and to new individuals entering the organization. Unfortunately, they may also contribute to the team's failure to meet standards and goals.

Therefore, a leader must be ever vigilant and be able to recognize team members' disengagement early and intervene immediately. If a disengaged employee is left unaddressed, it is highly likely that the individual will expend a lengthy amount of time before ultimately making a decision to change circumstance by either reengaging or by leaving the organization. Also, if left unaddressed too long, it makes an individual's recovery more difficult. Through a leader's intervention, the individual may successfully recover and reengage with the organization.

Leaders can do so through a recovery event. Key actions that can be taken by leaders are redoubling the actions in the engagement phase:

- Ensure the support of the employee imperatives.
- Introduce task variety or broaden job scope.
- Offer opportunities to make the employee relevant by participating in project work, expanding skill set, or identifying a target job the individual aspires to attain and plan for it.
- Have honest and open discussions about underlying issues and plan how to resolve open concerns.
- Restate the meaning of the individual's work and the purpose of the organization.

Post-Employment Period

If an individual becomes disengaged and cannot be recovered, a separation becomes inevitable and the post-employment period begins. Regardless of circumstances, it is critical that the organization and HR leaders continue to respect and uphold the dignity of the individual throughout and after the separation process. If individuals leave an organization in good standing, they should be treated as alumnae through an informal network that becomes an additional recruiting pool for future hiring needs.

It is also important to realize that an organization's employees and former employees become informal spokespersons for an organization, even beyond their employment. If an individual is able to leave an organization with respect and a belief that the entire employment experience was positive, it minimizes any negativity that an ugly separation could produce, particularly given the immediacy of communication through social networks.

HR professionals must work diligently to assist leaders and employees as they traverse the life cycle before, during, and after their employment. Both organizational leaders and HR professionals have a significant role to play in an employee's life cycle. They must ensure their team members' engagement by reinforcing the positive aspects of the employment relationship, culture, and environment that support the employee imperatives. An individual's engagement must be developed positively in order to ensure an optimization of the individual's performance and human capital.

In addition, leaders must understand that people also experience life events that will affect their engagement and focus. These experiences may be cheerful, such as childbirth or a wedding, or misfortunate, such as a family death or a divorce. Leaders can sustain an individual's engagement through these events by acknowledging them and offering celebration or condolences as appropriate. Balancing an organization and individual's needs is difficult, but effective leaders should plan for the unexpected. Essentially, the life cycle becomes a continuous effort to ensure that a strong engagement dominates the individual's life cycle.

The Employer–Employee Relationship

In a previous vignette, an experienced HR manager stated that HR's mission was to protect the company from its employees. Some within and outside the HR field share this view. However, it is based on an assumption that as soon as people enter into an organization, they are no longer a talent source that can yield creative thoughts and committed efforts for the organization, but rather that they are conniving nonconformists who attempt to find any manner or method to take advantage of the organization and its good faith. In any case, it would be as naive to believe that all people are good with the best intentions as it is to believe that all people are bad with the worst intentions and that all organizations work in good faith.

HR professionals and business leaders must take a position from which to form their perspective and approach about how to develop the organization's relationship with its people. Choosing to view people as adversaries creates a constant constraint that condemns the organization to expending resources to observe and enforce standards so that all people are made to conform and adhere. This approach offers minimal impact to the organization's success unless when done to uphold ethical, moral, and legal standards. As discussed in the opening chapter, the relationship between employers and their employees is most likely at its lowest ebb in light of economic trends and events. Assuming an adversarial relationship with employees will surely drive a deeper wedge between the organization and its people, a solemn legacy for many great organizations.

Believing that individuals possess talent that an organization can benefit from leads to developing the talent and its human capital for the betterment of the organization and the individual. It is for these reasons that organizations must define their culture and values not arbitrarily but rather by how they wish to define their relationship with stakeholders. Ignoring this dynamic leaves a relationship open for third-party representatives and competitors who predatorily seek to exploit an underdeveloped employer–employee relationship. Conversely, a best defense against third-party entanglements is a well-developed employer–employee relationship.

For example, when an employer–employee relationship is underdeveloped, defending and prevailing against a union organizing effort is a fifty-fifty outcome at best. Labor attorneys and management are forced to wage a campaign that vilifies unions. This strategy misses the underlying motive that employees, whether through honest or deceitful means by union representatives, see a failing in their employer–employee relationship. The union has presented itself as a better option on its own merits and to the detriment of the employer. By focusing exclusively on demonizing the union, the defensive effort overlooks the organization's exclusive advantage: its relationship with its employees. But as explained in some cases, union vilification is the legal and management team's only strategy as the organization's relationship with its employees is, at best, poor.

A strong employer–employee relationship is also a key factor in outperforming an organization's competitors, who are continuously seeking opportunities to gain a market advantage. Competitors often emulate market leaders; this may lead to an attempt to poach ideas and talent. Employees that are discouraged or disengaged are almost always able to find a willing competitor to lure them away. Whereas a well-developed employer–employee relationship promotes productivity and innovation, it also engenders a level of loyalty and protection.

Thereby, the employer–employee relationship serves as a competitive advantage only if it is developed and leveraged throughout the organization and the employee's life cycle. Honoring and satisfying the employee imperatives and observing and interceding when an employee wanders off the path of engagement further sustains the relationship. Furthermore, the organization must promote the positive aspects of its employer–employee relationship through communication of common interests, values, successes, and concerns. Doing so reinforces engagement, loyalty, and may help withstand business strategy shifts that create change or require adaptation. Additionally, nurturing the organization's relationship with people to foster individual and organizational success can have a greater influence than money or promotion opportunities on individual performance and retention.

Design Phase

Design the elements to influence and sustain a culture of people engagement to produce optimal outcomes.

186

Organizational culture can be a product of the values and beliefs that are demonstrated and reinforced by an organization's people in their response to circumstances, events, or other influences. Each organization has a culture whether or not it can be described. It can be assumed that an organization's customers influence its culture. When customers purchase or fail to purchase an organization's products or services, an organization's culture is driven by affirmation or exasperation. HR/OD professionals have been challenged by their assumed role of cultural designer when in fact a culture is less about deliberate design and more about a result of accepted behaviors and relationships. HR/OD professionals must work with other organizational leaders to understand what values and beliefs best enable the organization to successfully execute its strategy and enable people to produce optimal outcomes. A culture can be influenced by reducing undesirable behaviors and relationships and reinforcing model behaviors and relationships to sustain organizational success. Most critical to this point is leadership.

Leaders invariably model the behaviors and develop the relationships an organization's people maintain with the organization, the leader, and fellow employees. By understanding the employee imperatives, employee life cycle, the employer–employee relationship, and employee insight to optimal performance, senior leaders can establish the cultural foundation that can enable employees to create optimal outcomes and deliver on customer needs. For example, if employees produce their best results in an organization that communicates often with them, then communication becomes a necessary value and behavior in the organization. This should further drive designing programs that reinforce communication. In addition, there may be values or behaviors that are not critical to creating optimal outcomes directly but that meet societal standards with regard to moral and ethical behavior such as community involvement.

Implementation Phase

Refer to the implementation discussion presented in Principle #6.

Optimization Phase

Sustaining individuals and their relationship with the organization is essential. Employee engagement surveys can be used to measure engagement and to identify improvement opportunities. Even with best efforts in measuring a positive culture, people can become disengaged in their role, resulting in a diminished value of their human capital. Also, people may physically be separated from their role in the organization as a planned event (promotion, transfer, termination, etc.) or an unplanned event (resignation, injury, illness, etc.). The disengagement or loss of an individual in either manner causes the organization to incur a substantial direct and indirect cost. This loss creates demands or interruptions along the value chain that negatively impact the organization's efforts. Too often, their loss is simply accepted as a happenstance with minimal effort to study and reduce it. Organizations and HR teams must recognize this as a risk to the organization. How HR professionals and teams manage this risk directly impacts the sustainability of people and their human capital.

In reality, HR professionals manage risk on a daily basis. Invariably, every action or decision made by the organization or its employees contains an element of risk to that organization. Risk occurs from individuals physically working and producing outcomes (occupation), developing relationships with one another (interaction), creating and protecting intellectual capabilities (capital), and possessing the appropriate skills for the business situation (capabilities). Consider the following examples of people risk:

- A company operating a manufacturing plant within a profitable market that experiences an unusually high number of accidents
- A demotivated contact center employee provided with the best facilities, equipment, training, and resources available, arguing with another employee and being heard clearly by a customer on the phone

- A conscientious construction worker asked to help the organization in its shift from building residential homes to commercial buildings, without prior training, violates a building code, resulting in fines

Risk can impact the employment relationship with individuals or the organization's capability to compete successfully. The chart that follows categorizes the areas that harbor people risk.

Figure 3. People-Related Risk Areas

Employment Related		Organization Related	
Standards	**Legal/Regulatory**	**Operational**	**Strategic**
Policy	Federal/State Law	Productivity	Profitability
Ethics	Federal/State Agency	Turnover	Market Reputation
Morals and Values		Third Party Representation	Intellectual Capacity

How the HR leader perceives risk, whether adversely or favorably, has consequences that can either add a value or cost to the organization. Risk can be either a positive opportunity or it can be a peril for the organization. HR leaders must embrace their role as "people risk managers" to recognize and optimize the opportunities and minimize the perils in their broader effort to enhance human capital optimization efforts.

HR leaders must be adept at identifying and assessing all potential risks while making decisions, building programs, setting policies, and developing structures and processes at both the individual employee and the organizational level. Actions taken regarding an individual employee or team or the development of an organizational policy, process, program, or system contain inherent risks that impact the likelihood of achieving an organization's strategy.

Assessing risk requires an evaluation of a situation, decision, or action's characteristics:

- What are the potential risk areas and how is the risk defined and measured?
- Is the risk obvious or unclear and undeveloped?
- Is the risk relevant or unimportant to the ongoing organizational goals?
- What is the scope of impact to the organization?
- Is the risk short lived or will it be long lasting?[39]

Based on such a risk assessment, HR leaders must judiciously make a decision to address the risk if necessary while understanding the implications of doing so. One method to address risk is to completely eliminate it through a risk-avoidance approach.

In the people risk examples presented above, a risk-avoidance solution to the high-accident plant is for the company's leaders to close the plant so as to prevent any further accidents, thus avoiding the risk altogether. For the employee who did not have the knowledge and the employee who behaved badly, the company's leaders can terminate their employment.

However, the risk-avoidance approach in each of these scenarios is unreasonable. Given the plant's profit opportunity and the cost of losing an employee's human capital, risk avoidance can be a costly venture. Realistically, organizations and HR leaders must consider assuming a certain level of risk when the reward or return of doing so is greater than the risk. This requires risk management.

Managing risk requires an understanding of the underlying causes through investigation, developing solutions to eliminate or minimize the causes, and then implementing the solutions. Risk management is integral to an organization's effort to succeed. Therefore, HR professionals must consider adding risk management as a competency in order to maintain awareness of the most relevant risks. As HR leaders counsel management on employment or organizational matters, being competent with risk management in the context of the new doctrine is a necessity. In support of this effort, HR should develop a people risk profile that it routinely reports on to the organization's leadership.

By providing a greater focus on risk, HR professionals can proactively design an organization's infrastructure to minimize it and create a decision-making process to address it when identified. Managing risk to reduce exposure and promote reward is a contributing variable in sustaining an organization's human capital. In addressing risk, risk management initiatives may include the following:

- Develop engaging programs and practices to promote and protect employees from illness or injury through health and safety functions and wellness programs.
- Establish processes and policies to preserve the organization's intellectual knowledge and competitive capabilities for organizational learning and agility.
- Establish communication programs that promote stronger employer–employee relationships in order to encourage optimal outcomes and refute union threats.
- Create a proactive employee-relations strategy of outreach to prevent issues rather than a reactive ER strategy to resolve problems with a punitive approach.

The sustainability of people as a resource is essentially people risk management. Protection from physical harm or injury is paramount to organizational success. Recovery from absences due to health or injury must be deliberate and effective. Intellectual preservation through the documenting of processes, decisions, and actions that directly relate to an organization's competitive advantage is essential. Engaging people through communication and initiatives is key to retaining talent in the organization given the transient labor market of the new economy. Strong employer–employee relationships guard against third-party

threats, competitor poaching, and employee sabotage. If HR professionals can identify, assess, and manage people risk effectively, they can
ensure that through their efforts, people can be sustained as a deliverable to the organization in support of the optimization and deployment
of its people.

Chapter 4

Conclusion

John, the VPHR, turned off his office light and closed the door to end his day. It had been a day of great satisfaction. As he walked down the two flights to the parking garage, he could not help but smile with a heavy sigh.

Months earlier, he had joined an organization that resembled an uncontrollable wildfire with no relief. The organization's leaders and employees held the HR department in low regard. Management perceived HR's leaders as obstacles as they were consistently working against organizational leaders in their decision making. The employees saw HR as bureaucrats that took no interest in them as individuals and treated them indifferently. Morale was low.

Upon arriving, John first met with department leaders and employee focus groups to determine what their experience and expectations were for HR. He also met with the CEO, CFO, and COO to understand the organization's strategy and objectives. Finally, he met with the HR team to understand their experiences, expectations, systems, tools, and processes. He assessed the gaps between HR's expectations and those of their constituents. Armed with the CEO's vision and his newfound knowledge of the current situation, he began to form his plan to make HR a valued and highly respected resource.

This day, three months into his plan, a department head had come to his office to mention that he was noticing his managers having a much better relationship with HR and improvements were being made to his operation. Also, an employee came to his office to say thank you for the HR team going above and beyond with his benefits issue. Finally, as John stopped by the CEO's office for his day's last duty, the CEO said, "Thank you. We're finally starting to see a positive change and ideas are flowing again."

Given the economic circumstance, HR leaders and professionals are on the threshold of the HR field's third transformation. The complexity of managing an organization through the post–Great Recession era opens the door for a new HR doctrine and its principles. The doctrine does not present ready-made solutions for a broad range of HR issues that currently challenge HR leaders and teams in their daily strife. Notable issues that are not addressed in this writing include the challenges of social media in the workplace, the perpetual rising costs of healthcare, the change of demographics highlighted by the aging of the Baby Boomers, the war for talent, and the shifting compliance demands of both federal and state laws. Nor does the doctrine fundamentally change how HR performs its tasks and duties. The intent of introducing the new doctrine is to provide a new platform of perspective and thinking. A new platform that shifts HR's emphasis from its long and storied past of administrative and transactional preeminence to a promising and optimistic future dominated by a customer-facing, resource-driven approach.

In that future, HR leaders and teams will be looked upon to provide unprecedented expertise in how people are acquired, developed, deployed, optimized, and sustained in conjunction with an organization's business strategy and financial goals. Despite the criticisms presented in this book about the HR field, they are not aimed at HR's functionality, but rather at its approach, its application, and its unfulfilled potential for being a strategic contributor to many organizations. The presentation of a new HR doctrine presents an alternative path for HR professionals.

On this path, new HR professionals that enter into the field will continue to be positioned in specialty roles to develop baseline KSAs and competencies but also be afforded the opportunity to participate in one or more cross-functional HR deliverable teams. This provides these individuals a broader exposure to operational HR in the formative years of their career and also gives them a broader base of intellect and perspective in delivering HR's services. HR professionals will then be challenged to grow their expertise outside of HR by attaining business knowledge through formal study or by other means available to them. Emerging HR leaders tasked to assume responsibility for an HR deliverable will leverage their expertise and business acumen to garner necessary resources, guide teams with a strategy and plan, and execute the processes and practices to ensure acceptable results. Success will be measured by an organizational standard in achieving the strategy and goals as mentioned. HR scorecards will be less about measuring HR activity and more focused on the organization's people KSA and competency mastery, performance optimization, and risk containment in relation to customer satisfaction and financial results tied to revenue generation, cost containment, and earnings targets. When issues or problems arise, all HR professionals will be well versed in a process-improvement methodology. They will be able to identify and resolve underlying causes and improve the procedures or programs required to sustain HR's forward-moving pace in achieving its strategy.

The post–Great Recession work environment will continue to evolve as organizations attempt to find their way to a more secure and profitable future while dealing with relentless change. Not unlike the challenges hurled at organizations during the Industrial Revolution, the collapse of the economy in 1929, the transition to a wartime economy in the 1940s, the start of the technological era in the 1960s, or during the proliferation of investment activity in the 1980s, most organizations will either evolve and succeed or they will succumb and fail. Over the past decades, countless organizations had to do this to survive. For example, Xerox transformed from a copier company to a document company and IBM transformed from a computer company to a solutions company. Beyond simply rebranding themselves, these organizations transformed how they thought about the markets and customers they served as well as the products they offered.

Business functions, such as HR, can also transform in this manner. As mentioned at the beginning of this book, the workplace realities facing HR and organizations are as follows:

- Diminished human capital advantages as a result of low employee engagement and commitment levels.
- Organizational momentum toward strategic achievement interrupted by the transient nature of talent.
- Third-party resurgence from within the organization will develop if employee perceptions are not addressed.
- Employee litigation will continue to increase if relationships are not developed.

By shifting its focus to the organization's customer and the organizational constituents that create value for the customer, the HR function can evolve to address these realities. By unleashing its potential in a new way of thinking (ethos), through a broader knowledge base and by utilizing customer-focused designs and methods (praxis), the HR function can liberate itself from the chains of the institutional HR standard. HR professionals can immediately influence a shift in how HR operates that will reverberate throughout an organization by eliminating the bureaucracy and obstructions dictated by staid beliefs and assumptions that have frustrated both HR and its constituents throughout the years.

In this shift, HR's selfless ethos and advocacy of organizational success refocuses HR's view of its role within the organization and with people. People are perceived as a valued resource nurtured as talented individuals whose human capital can be optimized for both individual and organizational success. Setting aside disassociated agendas to become engaged with the organization and its people leads to an unleashing of the human spirit and potential and it ushers in a new age of HR's evolution.

An enriched affinity for people with an apt understanding of businesses and organizations enables HR professionals to execute their purpose to optimize the organization's talent and human capital. This includes rejecting the convenience of viewing people as inanimate file records or conniving individuals and resetting HR in a framework to align with the organization and its customer base. A renewed HR praxis turns HR's countenance outward from its own circumstances.

Designing and executing HR with the end in mind supplants HR's pre-dominant function-centric focus to ensure that the customers' and constituents' needs are melded into the HR strategy, structure, and methods. HR becomes less about avoiding risks and more about finding opportunities to succeed. HR compliance with laws and regulations is still a critical task, but lawmakers created these legal directives to ensure that people are valued and protected. Valuing and protecting people, as a resource, to promote success is an implied underlying driver of the strategic imperative of human capital optimization.

In a conversation about HR's role in organizations, Kimberly-Clark chief strategy officer and treasurer Nancy Loewe offered a financial leader's perspective by saying that HR leaders have to "define the people/talent objective." Loewe elaborated by further stating, "HR needs to help break that down into specific goals and strategies that relate to the business" and define "what success of the organization's people/talent objective will look like for the organization and for each function. The more specific, the better," she added.

Regardless of how history proceeds, HR is on the precipice of change that will entail how the people and talent objective is defined. That change will either be driven by external or internal influences and action. "There is a time before every change when people believe it is impossible; then, after change occurs, people believe that it was inevitable."[40] The opportunity to drive the change is in HR's hands. Reengineering the HR effort to serve the organization more effectively under the new doctrine prepares HR leaders and their staff both to keep and strengthen their seat at the table and to address the challenging realities of the new economy. The time is now for HR to do the impossible by considering a new doctrine, because a change in how HR integrates with an organization is inevitable.

Some within the HR field will challenge the transformative nature of this doctrine and its principles and reject its implications. Immersed in the administrative and transactional role to which they have become accustomed, many HR professionals may be satisfied with the status quo.

HR may be its own biggest obstacle in transforming itself. However, organizations and business unit leaders are growing impatient.

The HR leaders' challenge will be to engage each HR team member and align each HR activity with the effort to optimize and sustain people and their human capital. This becomes contingent upon the organization's readiness, the business leader's willingness, and the HR team's potential as enablers of this HR effort. HR leaders will have to clearly articulate HR's doctrine, purpose, structure, and effort and its alignment with the organization for HR to become a more valued partner. HR must continue to develop the center of excellence aspect of each HR function so that its advancement and best practices are continuously sought after and applied within the doctrine and strategy.

Ultimately, optimizing and sustaining human capital is to be driven by all HR professionals. Becoming intimately familiar with how an organization succeeds with its people and being a champion of that relationship is HR's future. There are many possibilities, many paths, and many existences that could become the new HR reality, but regardless of how HR will evolve, it will still be about people.

Notes

1   James Jacoby and Jill Landes, "House of Cards," CNBC, February 2009.

2   Mark Carlson, "A Brief History of the 1987 Stock Market Crash with a Discussion of the Federal Reserve Response," Board of Governors of the Federal Reserve, Washington DC (November 2006) 3–4.

3   Sarah Van Allen, "Customer Engagement: What's Your Engagement Ratio?" Gallup Consulting, 2009.

4   Michelle Conlin, "Is Optimism a Competitive Advantage?" *Bloomberg Businessweek*, August 13, 2009. http://www.cnbc.com/id/28892719

5   Fareed Zakaria, "The Future of Innovation: Can America Keep Up?" *Time* magazine, June 5, 2011.

6   Roy Maurer, "Report: Employment Practice Claims, Jury Awards Skyrocket." Society for Human Resources Management, December 20, 2012. http://www.shrm.org/Pages/login.aspx? ReturnUrl=%2fh rdisciplines%2femployeerelations%2farticles%2fpages%2fjuryawa rdsskyrocket.aspx.

7   Dave Ulrich, *Human Resource Champions: The Next Agenda for Adding Value and Delivering Results* (Boston: Harvard Business Review, 1996).

8   Karl Moore, "Dave Ulrich on Why HR Should Be at the C-Suite Table," *Forbes* magazine, 2011.

9   Keith Hammond, "Why We Hate HR," *Fast Company*, 2007.

10 Patricia Sellers, "Marissa Mayer: Ready to Rumble at Yahoo," *Fortune*, October 29, 2012.

11 Doc Searles, "The Customer as a God," *The Wall Street Journal*, July 2012, 21–22: sec. C: 1-2.
12 Patrick M. Wright, Timothy M. Gardner, and Lisa M. Moynihan, "The Impact of HR Practices on the Performance of Business Units," *The Human Resources Management Journal,* vol. 13 no. 3 (2003): 21–36.
13 FM 6-22, *Army Leadership: Competent, Confident, and Agile*, October 12, 2006.
14 Louis Fischer, *The Life of Mahatma Gandhi* (New York: HarperCollins, 1997).
15 Herbert Sloan, *The American Presidency: George Washington*, eds. Alan Brinkley and Davis Dyer (New York: Houghton Mifflin, 2004).
16 Doris Kearns Goodwin, *Team of Rivals* (New York: Simon & Schuster, 2005).
17 Sue Shellenbarger, "Showing Appreciation at the Office? No, Thanks." *The Wall Street Journal*, November 21, 2012: sec. D:3.
18 Joshua Lawrence Chamberlain, *The Passing of the Armies*, (New York: Bantam Books, 1993).
19 Steven Balsam, PhD, *Executive Compensation: An Introduction to Practice and Theory* (Scottsdale: World at Work Press, 2007).
20 Ibid.
21 W. P. Anthony, P. L. Perrewe, and K. M. Kacmar, *Strategic Human Resource Management*, 2nd ed. (USA: Dryden Press, 1996).
22 Boston Consulting Group, *The Product Portfolio*, 1970.
23 Igor Ansoff, "Strategies for Diversification," *Harvard Business Review*, vol. 35 issue 5 (Sept.- Oct. 1957): 113–124.
24 Michael Porter, *Competitive Advantage*, (New York: Free Press, 1985).
25 Steven Balsam, PhD, *Executive Compensation: An Introduction to Practice and Theory* (Scottsdale: World at Work Press, 2007).
26 Michael Porter, *Competitive Strategies: Techniques for Analyzing Industries and Competitors* (New York: The Free Press, 1980). W. P. Anthony, P. L. Perrewe, and K. M. Kacmar, *Strategic Human Resource Management*, 2nd ed. (USA: Dryden Press, 1996).

28 Ibid.

29 Ibid.

30 Ibid.

31 Ibid.

32 Ibid.

33 Ibid.

34 Ibid.

35 Steven Balsam, PhD, *Executive Compensation: An Introduction to Practice and Theory*, (Scottsdale: World at Work Press, 2007).

36 J. B. Quinn, *Intelligent Enterprise: A Knowledge and Service Based Paradigm for Industry*, (New York: Free Press, 1992).

37 Peter S. Pande, Robert P. Neuman, and Roland R. Cavanagh, *The Six Sigma Way Team Fieldbook: An Implementation Guide for Process Improvement Teams*, (McGraw-Hill, 2002).

38 Rachel Emma Silverman, "Algorithms Upend the Way Workers Are Paid," *Wall Street Journal*, (September 20, 2012), sec. B:1.

39 Russ Banham, "ERM: Viewing Risk as Opportunity," *Wall Street Journal*, (April 21, 2009). http://www.zurichna.com/NR/rdonlyres/DC2825DC-4892-4CEA-89FB-4ACF14D90757/0/WallStreetJournalPerspectivesonManagingRisk.pdf

40 Eugene Jarecki, *The Daily Show*, October 16, 2012. http://www.the-dailyshow.com/full-episodes/tue-october-16-2012-eugene-jarecki

Made in the USA
Charleston, SC
09 January 2014